Penobscot River

42 Castine

Cape Cod

The War in the North

This map is based on a modern survey.

No.	DATE	BATTLES	AMERICAN FORCES			BRITISH FORCES		
			COMMANDERS	ENGAGED	LOST	COMMANDERS	ENGAGED	LOST
	1775							
1	April 19	LEXINGTON & CONCORD	Parker, Barrett, & Heath*	3,763 in all	49k & 41w	Lord Percy & Lt. Col. Smith	1,800	73k & 174w
2	June 17	BUNKER HILL (Breed's Hill)	Gen. Putnam, Cols. Prescott & Stark	about 2,000	140k, 271w, 30c	Gens. Howe, Pigot, & Clinton*	2,400	226k & 828w
3	Sept. 5 to Nov. 2	SIEGE of ST. JOHNS	Gen. Richard Montgomery	1,200 to 1,500		Major Charles Preston	725	725c
4	Oct. 17	FALMOUTH	Town bombarded & burned by 2 British warships under Capt. Henry Mowat. 417 buildings & 11 vessels destroyed; 4 vessels taken.					
5	Oct. 25	MONTREAL	Ethan Allen	110	about 40c	General Guy Carleton	235	
6	Dec. 31	ATTACK on QUEBEC	Gen. Montgomery, Col. Arnold	800	60k & w, 426c	General Guy Carleton	1,800	5k & 13w
	1776							
7	May 15-20	THE CEDARS	Butterfield & Sherburne	540	400c	Captain Forster	640	
8	June 8	TROIS RIVIERES	General William Thompson	2,000	160k & w, 236c	Gens. Carleton & Fraser	6,000	8k & 9w
9	Aug. 27	LONG ISLAND	Gens. Washington, Putnam, Sullivan, & Stirling	about 3,500 out of 19,000	1,100w or c	Gens. Howe, Clinton, Grant, Cornwallis, & Heister	about 17,000 out of 32,000	63k, 314w & 23c
10	Sept. 15	KIP'S BAY	Colonel William Douglas	about 900		Howe, Clinton, & Cornwallis	4,000 plus	about 12k & w
11	Sept. 16	HARLEM HEIGHTS	Washington, Greene, Putnam	about 2,000	30k & 100w	General Alexander Leslie	about 5,000	14k & 157w
12	Oct. 11-13	VALCOUR ISLAND	Gens. Benedict Arnold & David Waterbury	750 men in 15 vessels	80k & w and 11 vessels	Gen. Guy Carleton & Captain Thomas Pringle	1,670 men in 20 vessels	about 40k & w and 3 vessels
13	Oct. 18	PELL'S POINT	Colonel John Glover	750	8k & 13w	Gens. Howe & Cornwallis	4,000	at least 25k & w
14	Oct. 22	MAMARONECK	Colonel John Haslet	750	3k & 12w	Major Robert Rogers	428	several k, w, 36c
15	Oct. 28	WHITE PLAINS	Gens. Washington, McDougall	about 1,600 out of 14,500	28k & 126w	Gens. Howe, Leslie & Heister	about 4,000 out of 14,000	313k & w
16	Nov. 16	FORT WASHINGTON	Colonel Robert Magaw	2,900	53k, 96w, 2,818c	General Knyphausen	8,000	78k & 374w
17	Dec. 26	TRENTON	General Washington	2,400	4w	Colonel Johann Rall	1,400	22k, 92w, 948c
	1777							
18	Jan. 3	PRINCETON	General Washington	about 4,000	30k & 75w	Lt. Col. Charles Mawhood	1,200	60k, 150w & 244c
19	April 27	RIDGEFIELD (Danbury Raid)	Arnold, Wooster, & Silliman	700	20k & 80w	Tryon, Agnew, & Erskine	2,000	154k & w, 40c
20	June 26	METUCHEN	General Lord Stirling	2,200	12k, 50w & 50c	Gen. Charles Cornwallis	4,000	70k & w
21	July 7	HUBBARDTON	Colonel Seth Warner	730	41k, 95w & 234c	Gens. Fraser & Riedesel	1,030	60k & 148w
22	July 8	FORT ANN	Cols. Long & Van Rensselaer	550	several k&w, 30c	Lt. Col. John Hill	190	13k, 23w & 15c
23	Aug. 2-23	SIEGE of FORT STANWIX	Cols. Gansevoort & Willett	750		Lt. Col. St. Leger & Jos. Brant	1,875	
24	Aug. 6	ORISKANY	Gen. Nicholas Herkimer	860	about 200k & w	John Butler & Joseph Brant	about 1,000	about 150k & w
25	Aug. 16	BENNINGTON	Gen. Stark & Col. Warner	2,330	30k & 50w	Lt. Cols. Baum & Breymann	1,442	207k & 700c
26	Aug. 22	STATEN ISLAND (Raid)	General John Sullivan	about 1,000	10k, 15w, & 140c	Gen. John Campbell	about 3,000	259c
27	Sept. 3	COOCH'S BRIDGE	General William Maxwell	720	about 40k & w	Lt. Col. Ludwig von Wurmb		at least 30k & w
28	Sept. 11	BRANDYWINE	General Washington	11,000	200k, 750w, 400c	Howe, Cornwallis, Knyphausen	12,500	90k & 480w
29	Sept. 19	FREEMAN'S FARM (Saratoga)	Gens. Gates & Arnold & Colonel Daniel Morgan	about 3,000 out of 7,000	65k & 218w	General John Burgoyne	about 3,000 out of 6,000	600k, w, & c
30	Sept. 21	PAOLI	General Anthony Wayne	1,500	150k & w, 17c	General Charles Grey		4k & 5w
31	Oct. 4	GERMANTOWN	General Washington	11,000	152k, 521w, 400c	Gen. Sir William Howe	9,000	70k, 450w, & 14c
32	Oct. 6	FORTS CLINTON & MONTGOMERY	Gens. George & James Clinton	at least 600	25k & 227c	Gen. Sir Henry Clinton	2,100 out of 3,000	40k & 150w
33	Oct. 7	BEMIS HEIGHTS (2nd Saratoga)	Gens. Gates & Arnold & Colonel Daniel Morgan	about 9,200 out of 11,000	50k & 150w	Gens. Burgoyne, Fraser, & Riedesel	about 2,200 out of 5,700	176k, 250w, & 200c
34	Oct. 22	FORT MERCER (Red Bank)	Greene & Hazelwood	about 400	14k & 23w	Col. Carl von Donop	1,200	377k & w, 20c
35	Nov. 10-15	FORT MIFFLIN (bombardment)	Col. Smith & Maj. Thayer	450	250k & w	Gen. Howe & Adm. Howe	6 ships; btrys.	13k, 24w; 2 ships
36	Dec. 5-8	WHITE MARSH	Gens. Washington & Irvine	11,000	about 90k & w, 32c	Gens. Howe & Cornwallis	14,000	about 60k & w
	1778							
37	June 28	MONMOUTH	General Washington	about 11,000 out of 13,425	142k, 300w, & 37 died of sunstroke	Gen. Sir Henry Clinton	about 13,000	190k, 390w, 576d, 59 died of sunstk.
38	July 3	WYOMING	Colonel Zebulon Butler	360	about 300k or c	Colonel John Butler	900	3k & 8w
39	Aug. 29	QUAKER HILL (Newport)	General John Sullivan	1,500 out 5,000	30k & 137w	Gen. Sir Robert Pigot	3,000	38k & 210w
40	Nov. 11	CHERRY VALLEY	Colonel Ichabod Alden	at least 250	70k & 33c	Walter Butler, Joseph Brant	700	
	1779							
41	July 16	STONY POINT	General Anthony Wayne	1,350	15k & 83w	Lt. Col. Henry Johnson	625	20k, 74w, & 543c
42	July-Aug.	PENOBSCOT EXPEDITION	Gens. Lovell & Wadsworth & Capt. Saltonstall	1,000 men & 40 ships	474k, w, & c all 40 ships	Colonel Francis MacLean	600	13k & w
43	Aug. 19	PAULUS HOOK	Major Henry Lee	300	2k & 3w	Maj. William Sutherland	about 250	50k & w, 158c
44	Aug. 29	NEWTOWN (Elmira)	General John Sullivan	3,462	3k & 39w	J. & W. Butler & Jos. Brant	600 to 1,200	at least 12k
	1780							
45	Feb. 3	YOUNG'S HOUSE	Lt. Col. Joseph Thompson	450	14k, 37w, & 76c	Lt. Col. Chapple Norton	550	5k & 18w
46	June 7&23	SPRINGFIELD	Greene, Maxwell, Dickinson	at least 1,800	about 15k, 61w	General Knyphausen	5,000	about 150k & w
47	Oct. 19	KLOCK'S FIELD	Gen. Robt. Van Rensselaer	about 1,500		Sir John Johnson, Jos. Brant	about 1,000	
	1781							
48	Sept. 6	FORT GRISWOLD	Lt. Col. William Ledyard	164	85k & 60w	General Benedict Arnold	1,700	48k & 145w
49	Oct. 25	JOHNSTOWN	Colonel Marinus Willett	400	40k & w	Major John Ross	700	40k & w, 30c

*NOTE: Names of victorious commanders are shown in Italics
Casualties are indicated by the following initials: k=killed; w=wounded; c=captured & d=deserted

Map and table of battles by JOHN T. BRADWAY

a
National
Historical
Society
book

the Concise
Illustrated History of the

Stackpole
Books

American
Revolution

text by Joseph P. Cullen

art selected by Frederic Ray

THE CONCISE
ILLUSTRATED HISTORY
OF THE
AMERICAN REVOLUTION

Copyright © 1972 by
National Historical Society
Published by
STACKPOLE BOOKS
Cameron & Kelker Streets
Harrisburg, Pa. 17105

Printed in USA.

Library of Congress Cataloging in Publication Data

Cullen, Joseph P
   The concise illustrated history of the American
Revolution.

   "A National Historical Society book."
   Bibliography: p.
   1. United States--History--Revolution. I. Title.
E208.C85   973.3   72-6250
ISBN 0-8117-0421-1

Contents

**The War in the North
—map and chronology** Front Endpapers

The American Revolution 7

the beginning of the armed conflict at Lexington and Concord.

The Coming of the War 17

an examination of the causes of colonial grievances and British reactions.

The Opening Guns 27

real warfare breaks out around Boston as growing numbers of Americans gather to confront the British there.

The General Takes Command 35

George Washington, a forty-three-year-old Virginia militia colonel, becomes general of the ragtag colonials.

Spread of the War 45

the conflict boils over into the southern colonies as British seapower begins to tell.

From War to Revolution 53

Congress declares the colonies independent as the fighting becomes more widespread and peace efforts fail.

The Fight for New York   65

in which the largest British expeditionary force in history
chases Washington's army away from the lower Hudson.

The Perilous Winter   72

Washington delivers a setback to the British in his
crossing of the Delaware but then has to endure a bitter
winter in New Jersey.

Victory, Defeats, and Valley Forge   83

The Americans win a decisive victory at Saratoga but
then are set back in a series of battles around Philadelphia. Then comes the black winter at Valley Forge,
relieved by news of the French-American alliance.

The Sea War   95

Britain's mighty fleet dominates the seas, giving her
great mobility. But the Americans fight back with their
privateers.

Uncertain Years, 1778-80   101

With Philadelphia and New York secure but having lost
New England, the Middle Atlantic, and the Northwest,
the British decide to concentrate on the South and thus
begins the road to Yorktown.

"The Destiny of Millions"   113

With assistance from the French, the Americans bottle
up Cornwallis at Yorktown and compel his surrender.
The active fighting ends, followed by a peace treaty.

Suggested Readings   124

Index   125

The War in the South
—map and chronology   Back Endpapers

The American Revolution

$\mathcal{A}$**pril 19, 1775** dawned clear and cold. On the road from Boston to Lexington a British force, numbering between 700 and 800, marched on its way to Concord to "seize and destroy all the Artillery and Ammunition, Provisions,

Paul Revere rides to warn of the British raid on Concord. *(H. A. Guerber's "Story of the Thirteen Colonies")*

Tents, & all other military stores you can find." They had been marching most of the night unobserved, they hoped.

No sooner had they left Boston, however, than two couriers, Paul Revere, a silversmith by trade, and William Dawes, a young cordwainer and experienced express rider, mounted and rode hard for Lexington and Concord by different roads to sound the alarm that the British Regulars were coming to capture the supplies. Revere reached Lexington first and stopped to warn Samuel Adams and John Hancock, two radical leaders hiding out from the British, that if they stayed there they probably would be captured as the soldiers marched through. Shortly afterward Revere was captured by a British patrol, but Dawes and Dr. Samuel Prescott, who had been courting a girl in Lexington, continued on.

As the scarlet tip of the sun burst over the horizon, flushing the cloudless sky, the advance guard of six companies of light infantry commanded by Major John Pitcairn approached the small village green in Lexington.

Samuel Adams, firebrand of the Revolution. From painting after Copley. *(Courtesy Independence National Historical Park)*

On the green stood sixty or seventy armed minutemen, farmers mostly and dressed as such, in two uneven ranks, commanded by Captain John Parker. "Let the troops pass by," Parker ordered, "and don't molest them without they begin first."

Pitcairn, a seasoned Marine veteran and a patient, tactful Scotsman, was relieved to see only a handful of armed men, but he could not ignore them. If he continued his march on the Concord road he would expose his right flank to the armed civilians, and he was too good a soldier to take that risk. He ordered his six light companies into line of battle and advanced across the green. Parker, sensing the hopelessness of the situation and conscious of his responsibility as company commander, ordered his men to disperse. Some of them began to drift away.

Then **"the shot heard 'round the world"** was fired, from where and by whom will probably never be known. Pitcairn, who had ordered his troops not to fire unless fired upon, lost

John Hancock, bold radical and moving spirit in the Revolution. From painting by Samuel F. B. Morse after Copley. *(Independence National Historical Park)*

control of his men temporarily. The Redcoats fired at the dispersing rebels and rushed after them with the bayonet, despite Pitcairn's order to cease fire. When the rising east wind cleared away the acrid smoke, it revealed the green deserted except for the Redcoats and the rebel casualties. Eight Massachusetts men had been killed and two wounded; one British soldier and Pitcairn's horse had received minor flesh wounds.

Who fired the first shot? All the minutemen denied that it came from their ranks, but it must be remembered that it was to the Americans' advantage to make it appear that the British had started it. Pitcairn, an honest and efficient

Old engraving of "The Battle of Lexington" from painting by Alonzo Chappel.

The fight at Concord Bridge, April 19, 1775. From the painting by F. C. Yohn.

officer, reported that he did not give the order to fire and did not believe his men fired first. It is possible, of course, that one of his junior officers or men might have fired without Pitcairn's knowledge. It is also highly possible that the first shot came from someone not on the green at all, but hiding behind a wall or tree, or from the group of spectators in front of the tavern on the green, or even, as some maintained, from an upper window of the tavern itself. Whoever he was, he was certainly a poor marksman, which would seem to rule out the men on the green who had the advantage of point-blank range at the massed British troops.

Of more significance is the question of why Captain Parker and his men were on the green in the first place. At midnight they had agreed "not to be discovered nor meddle," but just a few hours later they stood boldly exposed on the open green. Parker, an experienced soldier, realized they were too few to halt the British advance, but if he had by any chance decided to make a stand he surely would not have exposed his men in the open like that. He would have placed them behind trees, fences, or houses, Indian style. Why, then, this peculiar maneuver?

The finger of suspicion points to wily Sam Adams, the tireless agitator and the dynamo who kept the revolutionary movement going when the interest of others flagged. He believed that to "Put your enemy in the wrong and keep him so, is a wise maxim in politics, as well as in war." Organizer of the Boston Tea Party and propagandist for the so-called Boston Massacre, Adams was adept at practicing what he preached. "It must come to a quarrel with Great Britain sooner or later," he wrote, "and if so, what can be a better time than the present?"

At this time the American cause was not going well and the rebel leaders believed that some dramatic incident was needed to fan the flames, provided, of course, that the British could be made to appear in the wrong. It would certainly seem logical, then, and in character for Sam Adams to suggest to the Reverend Jonas Clark, the undisputed political leader in Lexington, and one whom Captain Parker would undoubtedly obey, that if the minutemen were to appear armed on the green it might provoke the British into making a mistake. In any event, Adams was not surprised at what did occur. Fleeing in a carriage with Hancock when they heard the Redcoat volley, Adams exclaimed, "Oh! What a glorious morning is this," and few believe he was talking about the weather.

The British immediately regrouped and continued to Concord. By now the alarm had gone far and wide. Bells, guns, and drums called out the minutemen and the militia. Express riders passed the word from town to town: "To arms! To arms! The war has begun!" Men seized muskets and powder horns and streamed towards Concord. Most of the military stores had already been removed or hidden, but what was left was now hastily taken to the woods, concealed in barrels and attics, or buried in ploughed fields. When the British entered Concord the Americans retreated to Punkatasset Hill, just west of the North Bridge over the Concord River, and the Redcoats proceeded to search the town, leaving only a small force at the bridge. The number

The Old North Bridge at Concord today.
Note the minuteman monument at the end of the bridge.
(Photo by Keith Martin)

of rebels on the hill steadily increased—minutemen, militia, and unorganized volunteers, old men and young boys. Soon they were over 400 strong and becoming surly and impatient. Were they going to stand there and let the Redcoats burn the town? No. The order was given to march on the bridge. It was all over in a few minutes, as the Redcoats retreated. The British had three killed and nine wounded; the Americans, two killed and three wounded.

Unable to locate any significant amount of military stores, the British force regrouped and a little later started the dangerous march back to Boston. For the first mile or so the long column was not molested. Then all hell broke loose, and for the remainder of the march the Redcoats were subjected to a galling and demoralizing fire from both flanks and front and rear. Only about 400 rebels had been in the fight at the bridge, but as the day wore on the number increased to several thousand. They would shoot at the enemy column from behind fences, trees, barns, walls, from inside houses, then reload, hurry ahead, and shoot again. This was a strange, new type of warfare to the British, who were neither experienced nor trained for it. To them it seemed dishonorable, hiding and shooting at men in the open who could not even see their enemies. As one Redcoat wrote his family: "They did not fight us like a regular army, only like savages."

But the column staggered on, the dead lay where they fell, the wounded tried desperately to keep up, and by late afternoon they were hungry, thirsty, exhausted, and almost out of ammunition. No longer an orderly marching column, they were now just a mass of men crowding the road. Soldiers looted homes, shot the occupants, and ransacked taverns for food and drink. A British officer admitted "that we began to run rather than retreat in order . . . the confusion increased rather than lessened."

First blow for liberty. The running fight as the British column retreats to Boston. Artist unknown. *(U.S. Army photo)*

With any organization and leadership at all, the Americans probably could have destroyed or captured the entire British force. But this was not an American army; it was merely an armed mob, angry and vengeful, with each individual more or less on his own. There was no order, direction, or control; no objective except for each man to get a shot at the hated Redcoats. So the column was allowed to reach Boston that night, having suffered about 273 casualties; the rebels about 95. And as the disordered American militia milled about Cambridge that night, one of them wrote his wife, "Tis uncertain when we shall return. . . . Let us be patient & remember that it is in the hand of God."

The
Coming
of
War

What **had begun** as an intellectual and political revolt was now an armed rebellion, the consequences of which no one could foresee. How had it come to this? It probably began at Jamestown in 1607. For the most part, the people who migrated to the New World were rugged individualists who went their own ways and resented any interference or restraint. The nature of this New World—a wild, rough wilderness—encouraged, in fact demanded, this characteristic if the settlements were to grow and prosper. Then, as the colonies developed and spread along the east coast, the English Government tended to leave them to their own devices, its primary interest being in the passage of laws that protected the trade and industry of the mother country. The result was that the political relationship between England and the young colonies evolved too haphazardly. Bacon's Rebellion against the Royal Governor's autocratic rule in Virginia in 1676 pointed up the inability of the English constitution to provide intelligent and satisfactory government for the ever-increasing number of Englishmen

Indignant colonists burning the stamped paper. The British never enforced the Stamp Act as a result of the protests.

outside the realm. The great distance between the colonies and England, the mass influx of non-English peoples, the enormous extent of the American continent and the

conditions existing in it, automatically created political, social, and economic ideas and values, divergent from those of the mother country.

Thus, by the 1760's it seemed evident to many colonists that some dramatic events or startling occurrences which would emphasize these differences, some acts of provocation or unnecessary show of power and authority alone were needed to arouse a strong spirit of protest in the colonies. Once aroused, that spirit, if properly led and encouraged, would inevitably develop into a spirit of revolt should its demands not be met.

Then, in the 1760's Parliament passed the Stamp Act, which levied an internal tax on such things as legal documents and newspapers, and the Townshend Acts, which put a duty or external tax on the importation of glass, paper, dyes, and tea. The strong, united opposition to these laws took the mother country by surprise, so both were repealed, with the exception of the tax on tea. But these taxes succeeded in keeping the spirit of revolt alive, and led to the formation of a secret organization known as the Sons of

Liberty, begun by Sam Adams in Boston, which soon spread to the other colonies. Most of the members were extreme anti-British radicals, and they were not at all averse

The hated revenue stamps. *(From Smith Burnham's "The Making of Our Country")*

to rioting, looting, and other illegal activities. Under the leadership of Adams, the Massachusetts Assembly sent a circular letter to all the other colonies urging united action. King George III then ordered the Royal Governors to dissolve any assembly that endorsed the letter. Wholesale dissolutions followed, as many of the colonies agreed with Massachusetts, including Virginia, whose action was most significant. Most of the taxes would have hurt the commercial colonies, but would have had relatively little effect on agricultural Virginia. Yet when the governor dissolved the Virginia Assembly, the delegates proceeded to Raleigh Tavern and adopted a nonimportation, non-consumption agreement similar to those adopted by her sister colonies. Thus the landed gentry gave notice to the mother country that they would stand by the merchants and patriots of the commercial colonies when it came to the issue of rights and freedom, regardless of the economic impact.

Then a volcano erupted in Boston, under the skillful guidance of Sam Adams. On a cold, snowy night in March

The famed "Boston Massacre." Lunette by Constantino Brumidi in the Capitol in Washington.

1770 a band of rowdies and ruffians so assailed a small group of British soldiers with jibes and oyster shells that the "lobsterbacks" without orders fired into the mob, killing five and wounding six. Promptly labeled a "bloody massacre" by the radicals, the incident was made to serve as a constant reminder of British tyranny.

For the next few years, however, a spirit of calm rested uneasily over the colonies. But under the peaceful surface the indefatigable Adams was always at work. Believing further clashes with England to be inevitable, and having as his ultimate goal the independence of the colonies, he devised a system of committees of correspondence to tie together all the towns in Massachusetts—and Massachusetts would not be alone. Down in Virginia another group of radicals led by such men as Thomas Jefferson, Patrick Henry, and Richard Henry Lee, also organized committees of correspondence and called on the other colonies to follow suit. Thus a beginning had been made creating the necessary machinery for effectively promoting united action by the colonies in the event of another provocation, which was not long in coming.

In 1773 Parliament passed a tea act designed to help the

powerful and influential East India Company to dispose of its surplus tea by giving it a virtual monopoly of the trade, and allowing it to bypass the colonial merchants. In bypassing the merchants, the act did what Sam Adams and the other radical leaders had been unable to do. It united the conservatives and radicals in opposition to the mother country. When the first small cargoes of tea, consigned to

This painting by Howard Pyle shows (left to right) Thomas Jefferson, Richard Henry Lee, and Patrick Henry meeting in the Raleigh Tavern in Williamsburg, Virginia. (Howard Pyle's "Book of the American Spirit")

This old print shows the Port of Boston in 1768.
(From Bryant's "Popular History of the United States")

Boston, New York, Philadelphia, and Charleston, were not allowed to get into the market places, it was a shock to the promoters of the act. But when a band of men disguised as Indians boarded the tea ships in Boston the night of December 16, 1773 and dumped the cargoes into the water, the British ministry was outraged.

King George's government determined that Massachusetts must be punished for this illegal act. Consequently, the following spring Parliament rushed through a series of disciplinary measures known as the Coercive or Intolerable Acts. The most obnoxious of these, as far as the colonies were concerned, was the Boston Port Act, which closed the port of Boston to all trade until the tea was paid for. Intended to intimidate the colonists and to isolate Massachusetts from the other colonies, these acts actually had the opposite effect. They united the colonies in support of Massachusetts, which then called for a meeting of representatives from all the colonies to be held in Philadelphia in September 1774. With the exception of remote Georgia, all responded.

This assembly, since known as the First Continental Congress, surprised British officials. The major weakness of colonial opposition was believed to be an inability to unite on any issue, due to geographic factors, economic interests, and sectional distrust. Indeed, many of the leading colonists themselves doubted, because of petty differences and jealousies, that they would ever achieve unanimity. From

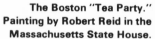

The Boston "Tea Party." Painting by Robert Reid in the Massachusetts State House.

the beginning it was clear that the Congress would be divided into two major factions, conservatives and radicals, one seeking compromise and reconciliation with England, the other urging defiance and united action which would probably lead to complete separation.

It was also soon evident that the success of any resistance movement against Parliament and the King would have to depend on a firm alliance between Massachusetts and

Carpenters' Hall in Philadelphia, where the First and Second Continental Congresses held their sessions. (*"Harper's Magazine,"* July 1896)

Virginia, who so far had been the leading exponents of opposition. Yet these two colonies were startlingly different in character and interests, and seemed on the surface to have nothing in common except their English ancestry. Virginia was run by an autocratic society of landed gentry whose power was founded on the plantation system which, in turn, was based on the institution of slavery. Massachusetts was, generally speaking, a democratic, middle-class society based on small, self-sufficient farms and a very active commerce, and controlled by lawyers and merchants. Any outward sign of disagreement between the delegates from these two colonies would undoubtedly cause the resistance movement to collapse.

King George III of England *(Collections of Library of Congres*

The leaders of the New England delegation, John Adams and his cousin Sam, were well aware of the dangers, and from the outset were determined to stay in the background, to let the Virginians have the floor, and the Virginians in turn agreed to work closely with the New Englanders in pursuit of their joint objectives. Although by no means ready yet even to suggest breaking off relations with the mother country, the radicals did succeed in getting the Congress to condemn the Intolerable Acts as unconstitutional, thereby countenancing resistance to them; to approve the arming of local militia; to adopt a nonimportation, nonexportation agreement called the Continental Association; to petition the Crown for a redress of grievances; and to pass the so-called Declaration of Rights, which reviewed the obnoxious measures passed by the Parliament and enumerated the fundamental rights the Americans believed themselves entitled to. It stated that these rights were derived from "the immutable laws of nature, the principles of the English constitution, and the several charters or compacts," and that among them was the right to "life, liberty, and property." The Congress agreed to meet again the following spring if no relief was forthcoming, and then adjourned.

King George ignored the petition of grievances, but news of the Association drew the ire of the whole British ministry. This was regarded as outright defiance which could seriously affect the entire British economy. "The New England governments," declared the King, "are now in a state of rebellion; blows must decide whether they are to be subject to this country or independent."

The Opening Guns

**Revolutionary Boston, with Faneuil Hall in the background.
Drawing by Howard Pyle.**

*T*his was the situation when in April 1775 General Thomas Gage, in command of the British troops in Boston, decided to try to capture two of the radical leaders, Sam

Adams and John Hancock, and to destroy the military stores believed to be hidden in Concord. He failed in both quests, and his force was driven back to Boston and placed under siege, while Hancock and Adams proceeded to the meeting of the Second Continental Congress in Philadelphia, which convened in May 1775. By now about 3,000 rebel militia were swarming about Cambridge on the outskirts of Boston. Massachusetts then appointed militia General Artemas Ward to command, and appealed to the other New England colonies for reinforcements to keep the British penned up in the city. The state also commissioned Captain Benedict Arnold, of the Connecticut militia, as a colonel in the Massachusetts militia and authorized him to raise a force of not more than 400 men from western Massachusetts and neighboring colonies to capture the lightly held British Fort Ticonderoga on Lake Champlain in upper New York. The incongruity of this situation was

The guns of Fort Ticonderoga still stand watch over Lake Champlain, British invasion route from the north. *(New York State Department of Commerce photo)*

apparently lost on the New Englanders—Massachusetts commissioning a member of the Connecticut militia to capture a British fort in the colony of New York.

On the way Arnold learned that Ethan Allen and his "Green Mountain Boys" from Vermont were also planning an attack on the fort. They combined forces and in May

Ethan Allen leads his "Green Mountain Boys" in the surprise capture of Fort Ticonderoga, routing out the British commander in his night clothes.

captured it, along with seventy-eight heavy pieces of artillery and a few mortars and howitzers. These were the guns that would eventually drive the British out of Boston.

When news of this victory reached Philadelphia the radicals were jubilant, but they were also worried. What worried them particularly was the army around Boston. Without Congressional support and control, without a commander in chief appointed by the Congress, the army might disband and go home, and with it would go the opportunity for independence. But who to appoint to allay the fears and distrust? Some thought old General Ward, an experienced military officer, should be left in command despite his age. It was argued that it might cause serious discontent and desertions among the New England troops, the only force in the field, if he were removed from command. But would troops from the other colonies, particularly the Southern, serve willingly and faithfully under a Massachusetts general? Many thought not. Some feared that a leader from the Middle Colonies might be more loyal to the King than to the Congress. Charles Lee, an eccentric English officer who had offered his services, was a likely candidate with some support among the delegates. He had the distinct advantage of not being from any one section or colony. But others, particularly John and Sam Adams, believed that the crucial command should go to a Southerner. Their choice was a fellow delegate from Virginia, Colonel George Washington, "a fine figure and of a most easy and agreeable address," wearing the handsome blue and red Virginia militia uniform.

There was opposition to this proposal, not because of any objections to Washington personally, but again because of sectional fears and distrust. The Virginians were known as radicals. For several days energetic lobbying was carried on, or as one delegate expressed it, "Pains were taken out of doors to obtain a unanimity." Finally on June 15 Washington was elected unanimously, in what was undoubtedly the second most significant decision made by the Congress, and as one delegate stated, the appointment "will be very agreeable to our officers and soldiery, it removes all jealousies, more firmly cements the Southern to the Northern and takes away the fear of the former lest an enterprising eastern New England General proving successful, might with his victorious army give law to the Southern or Western gentry." The Congress also voted to send ten companies of Maryland, Pennsylvania, and Virginia riflemen to Boston to make it a truly "Continental" army, and resolved that "a sum not exceeding two million of Spanish milled dollars be emitted by the Congress in bills of credit, for the defense of America."

Before Washington could reach Cambridge to take command, however, a major battle erupted in Boston. Gage, now assisted by Generals William Howe, Henry

John Trumbull's painting of the Battle of Bunker Hill. *(Courtesy of Yale University Art Gallery)*

Clinton, and John Burgoyne, realized that his situation in Boston was precarious, to say the least. If the rebels occupied Dorchester Heights to the south, or the heights of the Charlestown peninsula across the bay, Boston would be untenable. Consequently, Gage decided to occupy Dorchester Heights. When the Americans learned of this they decided upon an immediate countermove against the high ground on the peninsula. Under cover of darkness on June 16 a force of about 1,200 men commanded by Colonel William Prescott and General Israel Putnam moved quietly onto the peninsula and climbed to the top of Bunker Hill. Here, after a two-hour discussion, it was decided to build the main fortification on a smaller hill, later called Breed's Hill, a few hundred yards closer to Boston, and to erect only a secondary work on Bunker Hill. This, unfortunately, was a critical error as Bunker Hill could have been made almost impregnable, while the smaller elevation was vulnerable. Who was in actual command, Prescott or Putnam, has never been determined. At best, then, it was a divided command, subject to such errors.

Dawn revealed the hastily erected fortifications to the British, and the ships in the harbor immediately opened fire but with little effect. Gage realized he had to drive the Americans off the peninsula or evacuate Boston. He ordered a frontal attack to be conducted by General Howe with about 2,400 troops on June 17. Twice Howe's Redcoats stormed bravely up the hill in close formation, burdened by heavy packs weighing between 100 and 125 pounds, only to be blasted back by the murderous fire of the Americans who had been ordered not to shoot until the enemy was within about fifty yards. Reinforced by Clinton, Howe then ordered a third assault, only this time the packs were to be left behind, the troops were to hold their fire until close to the rebels, and immediately after firing were to follow up with a bayonet charge; this time the assault succeeded. As

Final British Assault on Breed's Hill. *(Drawing by Howard Pyle in his "Book of the American Spirit")*

the Redcoats charged up the hill the fire from the American fortifications slackened, because, incredibly, they were short of powder, none having been delivered from the rear during the fight. With no bayonets to defend themselves, the rebels were forced to flee.

The British victory, however, was extremely costly, particularly in the loss of officers. Out of about 2,400 engaged, Howe suffered over 1,100 casualties, about 45 percent. He reported sadly, "I freely confess to you, when I look to the consequences of it, in the loss of so many brave officers, I do it with horror. The success is too dearly bought." The Americans suffered only about 400 casualties. Although there was little in the way the battle was conducted for the rebels to boast about, there is no question that it had a major effect on the way the British generals acted for the remainder of the war. It was almost a year before they resumed the offensive, and never again did they act with the same speed, energy, and aggressiveness they showed at Bunker Hill.

Washington taking command of the army at Cambridge. ("Scribner's Magazine," Feb. 1898)

The General Takes Command

*E*arly in July Washington arrived in Cambridge to take command, not of an army, but of a loosely knit group of men now numbering something over 14,000. There was no unified command, little discipline, a lack of organization and supplies, and no plan for training. Washington was appalled, but also amazed at what these ragged rebels had accomplished. In his report to Congress he showed that he realized how they had done it. "The deficiencies in their numbers," he wrote, "their discipline, and stores can only lead to this conclusion, that their spirit has exceeded their strength." But more than spirit would be needed, as Washington well knew, if the Americans were to be successful, and he immediately set about the difficult task of organizing, disciplining, and training an army, and for this he needed time. Fortunately, the British gave him plenty. After the shock of Bunker Hill they seemed content just to sit in Boston and await reinforcements and orders. In September Gage was recalled and Howe was placed in command, but he too showed no inclination to take the offensive.

While Washington was thus engaged, the Congress received word that Sir Guy Carleton, military governor of Canada, was "making preparations to invade these colonies

Washington at his headquarters at Cambridge. Painted by H. A. Ogden. (Photo courtesy Kenneth M. Newman, Old Print Shop, NYC)

. . . and instigating the Indian nations to take up the hatchet against them." For generations the Canadian province had been both a threat and a temptation to the American

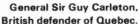

General Sir Guy Carleton,
British defender of Quebec.

colonists. New Englanders particularly remembered how the French had successfully used the rivers and lakes from the St. Lawrence to the Hudson as an avenue of invasion. Now they feared the British would use them the same way to separate the New England Colonies from the Middle Colonies. But other influential colonial leaders believed that if given support and an opportunity, the Canadians would join the rebellion and become the fourteenth colony. So in late June Congress ordered General Philip Schuyler to proceed to Ticonderoga and Crown Point and, if he found it

Daniel Morgan's Virginia riflemen lead the American invasion of Canada through the Maine wilderness. Painting by Stanley M. Arthurs.

practicable, and "not be disagreeable to the Canadians, he do immediately take possession of St. Johns, Montreal and any other parts of the country."

It was generally believed that Carleton had fewer than 800 regulars, and those so scattered as to be ineffective, and that he could not be reinforced until spring, at which time it was hoped the province would be securely in American hands, thus forestalling a British buildup for an invasion south. It was also calculated that once the main cities had been seized, the Canadians would willingly join in the fight for freedom. The invasion route selected was the traditional north-south avenue by way of Lake George and Lake Champlain to Montreal. Second in command of the 1,800-man force was General Richard Montgomery.

Brigadier General Richard Montgomery, able American commander who died in the assault on Quebec. *(New York Public Library Print Collection)*

General Sir William Howe, British commander in chief, who succeeded General Thomas Gage at Boston, but had to evacuate the town.

While this force was proceeding to Ticonderoga, Washington came up with another plan. Why not send another column at the same time to attack Quebec, just 150 miles down the St. Lawrence from Montreal? If the two cities were attacked simultaneously, Carleton would be at a serious disadvantage and in all probability could not defend both. A practicable route seemed to be open, up the Kennebec River, then along the Dead River to Lake Megantic and down the Chaudiere to where it met the St. Lawrence within four miles of Quebec. For this mission he selected 1,050 volunteers and picked riflemen under the command of Colonel Benedict Arnold.

Schuyler laid siege to St. Johns September 6; then, because of illness, relinquished command to Montgomery, an extremely able officer. The garrison capitulated November 2, but Carleton escaped with the remnants of his small force to Quebec, thereby uncovering Montreal, which the Americans occupied on November 13. Arnold's column, after suffering incredible hardships through brutal terrain and weather, reached the outskirts of Quebec November 9. By now the force consisted of only about 600 gaunt, ragged men, their clothing "torn in pieces . . . hung in strips—few had any shoes but moggasons made of raw skins—many without hats, beards long and visages thin and meager." Montgomery with 300 men joined Arnold, and on December 31 they attacked the walled city in a snowstorm, only to have the assault end in disaster when Montgomery was killed and Arnold wounded. Arnold, however, refused

Death of Montgomery in the attack on Quebec. Painted by John Trumbull. *(Courtesy Yale University Art Gallery)*

to give up. He appealed to Congress for reinforcements and decided to keep the remnants of his force around the city for the winter—a heroic gesture, perhaps, but a foolhardy one, fraught with suffering and danger for his men. Carleton was well supplied to withstand a winter siege, and with the coming of spring and more British troops he would have little difficulty in driving the Americans away. In the

meantime, Arnold's men suffered cruelly from the weather, smallpox, and hunger. The natives refused to feed them and Arnold admitted that "our credit extends no farther than our arms." The result was that the men plundered priest and peasant alike, despite Washington's orders to the contrary. Thus the attempt to win the support of the Canadians to the American cause was doomed.

King George, meanwhile, refused even to receive the so-called Olive Branch Petition, forced through the Congress by the conservatives, which affirmed their loyalty to the King, but reiterated the grievances of the colonies, and begged the Crown to prevent further hostilities until some compromise could be worked out. Instead the King now proclaimed all the colonies to be in open rebellion and prohibited all commerce with them, effective March 1, 1776. These actions, of course, considerably strengthened the hands of the radicals. "Now," wrote Jefferson, "we want neither inducement nor power to declare and assert a separation. It is will, alone, that is wanting, and that is growing apace under the fostering hand of our King."

Something soon came to build much of the will necessary, in the form of a forty-seven-page pamphlet entitled *Common Sense,* showing once again that perhaps the pen can be mightier than the sword. Written by Thomas Paine, a 38-year-old English immigrant, it was published in Philadelphia in January 1776 and within three months had sold over 100,000 copies, a phenomenal sale in that day and age. Despite its title, it appealed to the emotions rather than to reason, and it was not aimed primarily at the educated people. Paine had the ability to speak in the language of the ordinary colonist. He pleaded the cause of independence by ridiculing the theory of the divine right of kings, thus undermining respect for the Crown, by then really the last tenuous tie with the mother country. Even more important than his ridiculing of kings, was his clear call for immediate independence. "Everything that is right or reasonable pleads for separation. The blood of the slain, the weeping voice of nature cries, 'Tis time to part'." This was the message that spread throughout the colonies, the message that Congress with all its petitions and resolutions had not been able to get across to the ordinary colonist.

Then, as if the idea of independence needed a further

Thomas Paine, author of "Common Sense," Painting by Bass Otis. *(Photo courtesy Independence National Historical Park)*

stimulant, Parliament proceeded to give it the final push. It passed an act removing the colonies from the protection of the Crown, and authorizing the seizure and confiscation of all American ships at sea. Passed in December 1775, news of it reached Philadelphia at the end of February and threw the delegates into consternation. The radicals, of course, were delighted at this additional blunder. The mother country herself had now cut the colonies off and practically declared war. The conservatives, still fighting for reconciliation, found the ground cut from under them. But it would still take time, time for more debate, more doubts and soul-searching. This was no small thing that was now being contemplated. To throw off a monarchy in mid-18th century, to reject outright the theory of the divine right of kings with its strong religious overtones, was indeed an awesome step that brought inner fear and trembling to many. Down through the ages this form of government had seemed almost natural—the chief in the tribe, the father in the family image—with its symbol of law and order, of security and safety. It had endured through history, while democracies had been little more than strange interludes. Now it was being proposed that faith in this historic symbol be replaced with faith in the collective individualism of a republican democracy. It is small wonder that there was violent disagreement, and more time was needed. As Benjamin Franklin explained, "The novelty of the thing deters some, the doubts of success, others, the vain hope of reconciliation, many."

By now it was evident to the British Government that the plans for subduing the American colonies would have to be conceived on a much grander scale than had been at first anticipated. The strategy of simple seizure of certain towns and cities along the coast, which could be done because of British control of the sea, or of burning towns and dispersing small bands of ragged rebels, would not crush the revolt. Instead, a much broader plan was now developed. The decision was to divide the colonies and conquer them in big chunks in order to isolate the three general areas, that is, the New England Colonies, the Middle Colonies, and the Southern Colonies. Three large columns would do this, one moving south from Canada, another sweeping north from the Carolinas, and the third thrusting through New York and Pennsylvania and then splitting north and south to unite with the other two columns. It was a simple "divide and conquer" strategy that should have been successful. Its failure lay in lack of over-all support and coordination on both the political and military levels, and a critical underestimation of the ability and determination of the rebels on the part of the individual British field commanders.

$\mathcal{T}$**he first move** in this plan was made January 20 when Clinton sailed from Boston with a force he vaguely estimated at between 1,200 and 1,500. He was to rendezvous off Cape Fear, North Carolina with another command under General Lord Charles Cornwallis and Admiral Peter Parker to be sent from Ireland. Originally headed for

Spread
of the
War

Admiral Sir Peter Parker commanded the British fleet in its abortive attack on Fort Sullivan *(Fort Moultrie)*.

Charleston, South Carolina, the expedition changed its destination to Cape Fear because Governor Josiah Martin of North Carolina convinced the British that with the help of a few British regiments he could raise enough Loyalists to put down the rebellion in North Carolina first, and this, he

A Revolutionary period cannon looks out over the Moore's Creek battlefield. *(National Park Service photo)*

claimed, would facilitate the capture of South Carolina and Georgia. Martin based his hopes of raising a large force primarily on a relatively new group of immigrants, the so-called Highland Scots, who had made small settlements in several coastal counties. They had fought for the Stuarts against the House of Hanover in 1745, and after their bloody defeat at Culloden had found refuge in the New World. Although they had no love for the Hanoverian George III, they had still less for most settlers in the Piedmont area, many of whom were the so-called Lowland or Scotch-Irish immigrants.

Thus by 1775 North Carolina was generally split into two groups: the Patriots, consisting primarily of the Scotch-Irish and other settlers of the Piedmont, who favored independence from the Crown; and the Loyalists or Tories, primarily the Crown officials, wealthy merchants and planters, conservatives, and the Scots Highlanders, who favored loyalty to the King at any price.

The fleet from Ireland was supposed to sail in December, but in fact did not leave until the middle of February. As communications between Britain, General Howe, and Governor Martin were necessarily slow and unreliable, the governor decided to start raising his army without waiting for the arrival of the British troops. By February 15 he had about 700 Highlanders and 800 other Loyalists, under the command of 80-year-old Donald McDonald, an experienced soldier and general in the militia. But as soon as word of the Loyalist activities leaked out, the Patriots began gathering their forces under Colonel James Moore of the 1st North Carolina Regiment. Moore raised about 1,000 volunteers and minutemen and decided to contest the Loyalist march to the coast to join the Redcoats at Moore's Creek bridge, about twenty miles above Wilmington.

In the misty dawn of February 27 with drums beating and bagpipes skirling, the Highland Scots, some dressed in plaids and kilts, rushed the bridge, swinging the terrible claymores and screaming their battle cry, "King George and Broadswords!" They were met by a withering fire at point-blank range as rebel rifles flashed and cracked in the pale gray light. Almost the whole advance party was cut down. In less than five minutes the Loyalist force was in complete retreat, which quickly turned into a rout as the rebels promptly mounted a counter-attack. In the next few days they captured over 800 Loyalists, almost destroying that small army and preventing the rendezvous with the British. Although not realized at the time, this victory did much more than merely check the growth of Loyalist sentiment in the colony. It fanned the fires of revolutionary fervor to such a pitch that on April 12 North Carolina instructed its delegation to the Second Continental Congress in Philadelphia to vote for independence—the first colony to do so. It also thwarted the planned British

General Sir Henry Clinton. His force failed to support the naval attack on Fort Sullivan. (Kean Archives)

A 1774 view of Boston from Dorchester Heights.

invasion of North Carolina. When the British force finally arrived off Cape Fear, it moved on to the original destination of Charleston.

During the winter Washington had whipped his force into a fairly respectable army, and by March it numbered about 16,000 men. He now desired to take some offensive action before the British could be reinforced in the spring. His officers agreed but, believing the army was not strong enough to attack Boston, it was decided to occupy and fortify Dorchester Heights. By this maneuver they hoped to force the British either to attack or evacuate. The necessary artillery for such action was available, General Henry Knox having had it hauled laboriously by hand overland from Fort Ticonderoga during the winter. On March 4 under cover of darkness and artillery fire General John Thomas moved onto the Heights with 2,000 men and quickly threw up prefabricated fortifications, picks and shovels being useless on the frozen ground. By daylight the job was complete. "The rebels have done more in one night than my

Brigadier General Henry Knox, Washington's chief of artillery, who moved the "noble train of artillery" captured at Fort Ticonderoga to Boston. *("Magazine of American History," 1883)*

Tom Lovell's painting of the artillery train moving from Fort Ticonderoga to be placed on Dorchester Heights. *(Courtesy of John Dixon Crucible Co.)*

whole army could do in months," Howe is reported to have remarked when he viewed the fortifications. Realizing he would have to attack or evacuate and with the memory of Bunker Hill still fresh in his mind, Howe chose the latter. By

March 17 the British had sailed for Halifax, taking about 1,000 Loyalists with them.

Washington, however, was not deceived by this move. He anticipated that Howe's next attack would be against New York City, and he immediately moved his small army there. "It is the Place that we must use every Endeavor to keep from them," he wrote. "For should they get that Town, and the Command of the North River, they can stop the Intercourse between the northern and southern Colonies, upon which depends the Safety of America." Once in New York he put all available labor to work digging entrenchments and erecting forts, redoubts, and batteries.

The British evacuate Boston, March 1776. Painted by H. Charles McBarron, Jr. *(Courtesy of American Oil Co.)*

Colonel Moultrie and his 400-man garrison successfully defend Fort Sullivan. Painted by F. C. Yohn. *(Henry Cabot Lodge's "The Story of the Revolution")*

While Washington was thus engaged that spring, Clinton was finally joined by Cornwallis and Parker off Charleston early in May. Although ordered to join Howe later in New York, Clinton decided to attack Charleston before he sailed north. The entrance to the harbor was protected by forts on two islands, Fort Johnson on James Island, and Fort Sullivan (later called Fort Moultrie) on Sullivan's Island. The latter fort, however, was only about half built and consisted of nothing more than palmetto logs and sand, with the rear virtually open and undefended. Here, on June 28 Colonel Moultrie and about 400 South Carolinians withstood the fire of over 100 British naval guns and beat back Parker's attack of three ships of the line, damaging all of them and inflicting over 200 casualties on the British.

Clinton also failed miserably when he tried to support Parker's naval attack. He landed most of his troops on Long Island (later named Isle of Palms), near Sullivan's Island and separated from it by a channel called the Breach, which Clinton was led to believe was only eighteen inches deep. But when he tried to storm the rear of Fort Sullivan he discovered to his chagrin that in places the water was seven feet deep, and under a heavy fire he withdrew and abandoned the attempt. By nightfall it was all over, and the British force later sailed for New York. The Americans had suffered only about thirty-two casualties.

This humiliating British defeat, coupled with the failure of the Loyalists at Moore's Creek, kept the Southern Colonies free of British control for the next three years, enabling the rebels to send men and supplies to the Middle Colonies to support the American cause. As the noted historian Edward Channing stated: "Had the South been conquered in the first half of 1776 it is entirely conceivable that rebellion would never have turned into revolution. . . . At Moore's Creek and Sullivan's Island the Carolinians turned aside the one combination of circumstances that might have made British conquest possible."

From War to Revolution

*I*f the news from the South was encouraging, that from the North was not. In April Arnold's small force, which had spent the terrible winter in front of Quebec, was finally reinforced by Congress with enough troops to bring its strength up to about 2,000, and in May General John Thomas, a capable, energetic officer, was placed in

View of Quebec from Point Levy. Painted by Richard Short. *(From engraving by P. Canot in the Public Archives of Canada)*

command. Thomas immediately realized that the little army, racked by disease and desertions, was in no condition to conduct a siege. He ordered a retreat. While this move was underway, Carleton, now reinforced by regular troops from England, sallied out with a force of about 900 men and drove the Americans south in panic, a disorganized mob with little trace of any military system, "without order or regularity, eating up provisions as fast as they were brought in." By early July they were back on American soil at Fort Ticonderoga, and Montreal and Quebec were safe in British hands. Despite this failure of the Canadian campaign, it did achieve one of Washington's main objectives in delaying for over a year a British buildup for an invasion south.

"British Fleet Below Staten Island" June 18, 1776. Wash drawing by Archibald Robertson. *(Spencer Collection, New York Public Library. Astor, Lenox, and Tilden Foundations)*

As Washington had predicted, Howe's main objective now became the Middle Colonies. He sailed from Halifax and arrived at Staten Island, New York on June 25. His immediate goal was New York City, which he hoped to use

View of New York from the northwest, probably prior to 1773. Aquatint by Joseph F. W. Des Barres. (*Courtesy Edward W. C. Arnold Collection, Metropolitan Museum of Art*)

Passage of the British troops to Long Island. (*Bryant's "Popular History of the United States"*)

as his major base for the conquest of the colonies. Reinforcements arrived steadily. Within a week 130 ships of war and transports disembarked over 9,000 troops. On July 12 Admiral Richard Howe, brother of the general, arrived with a fleet of 150 ships crowded with soldiers fresh from England. A little later Parker arrived from Charleston with 2,500 men under Clinton and Cornwallis. In August they were joined by 8,000 German Hessians. Howe's total force now consisted of approximately 32,000 well-disciplined professional soldiers, fully armed, equipped, and supplied. This was the largest expeditionary force England had ever dispatched.

There was nothing Washington could do to prevent this powerful buildup. To oppose Howe's forces in the New York area he had about 19,000 effectives, many of them raw militia and most of them poorly armed, equipped, and supplied, led for the most part by amateur officers. Despite their handicaps these civilian soldiers now had something tangible and worthwhile to fight for—Independence. On July 2, after months of violent disagreements and debates, the Congress passed a resolution "That these United Colonies are, and of right ought to be, free and independent

States, that they are absolved from all allegiance to the British Crown, and that all political connection between them and the State of Great Britain is, and ought to be, totally dissolved." Introduced by Richard Henry Lee of Virginia and seconded by John Adams of Massachusetts, it was a fitting climax to the long alliance between Virginia and Massachusetts in the quest for independence.

The die was now cast; there could be no turning back. What was needed now was a formal document to proclaim the fact to the world, and at the same time to justify and

Thomas Jefferson, author of
the Declaration of
Independence.

explain the necessity for this world-shaking event. Thomas Jefferson had drafted a declaration, and July 3 and 4 were spent discussing it. The Congress went over it carefully, paragraph by paragraph, changing a word here, a sentence there, striking out this, adding that. The members rejected completely a severe censure of the people of Great Britain and they struck out Jefferson's caustic condemnation of the slave trade. In late afternoon July 4 the amended declaration passed, although it would not be signed by the members until a later date.

The Congress could truthfully title it the Unanimous Declaration, but it should not be inferred from this that the majority of the American colonists were necessarily in favor of it. The struggle for independence was as much a civil war as a revolution. It was not, of course, a contest between large sections of the country, but in every colony, county, town, and village it sometimes pitted father against son and brother against brother. Those who remained loyal to the Crown, the Tories or Loyalists as they were called, comprised a large group, possibly as many as one-third of the inhabitants. Over 75,000 of them left the country and some 30,000 fought in British regiments at one time or another. These figures are startling when it is realized that Washington never had more than 25,000 men in the field at any one time. Thousands of others fled across the Appalachians to avoid paying the taxes to finance the revolution. Many refused to sell supplies to the rebels for Continental dollars, but traded freely for British gold. And some tried to remain neutral, particularly in the beginning, until they could see how it would all come out in the end. There is nothing particularly surprising in this, of course, as revolutions seldom if ever are begun by majorities. A Congressional Committee believed that if the revolution failed it would be due to "such divisions more than to the force of our enemies."

The Pennsylvania State-house, where the Declaration was signed.

Tory refugees on their way to Canada. Painting by Howard Pyle in his "Book of the American Spirit."

Paper money of Revolutionary times.

Nor should it be surprising that the American people have made the anniversary date of the passage of the Declaration, rather than the Resolution, the national birthday. The Declaration did more than just declare independence. It stated in clear and succinct words a fundamental philosophy of government that has guided this Nation ever since; it not only declared men free, it stated *why* men should be free, and the reasons could be applied to every nation in the world. A political document, it was designed and written to justify an action already taken, and to help promote the American case for freedom. In this it succeeded admirably. As Washington stated when he ordered the troops assembled in New York to hear the Declaration read: "The General hopes that this important event will serve as a fresh incentive to every officer and soldier to act with fidelity and courage, as knowing that now the peace and safety of his country depends (under God) solely on the success of our arms; and that he is now in the service of a State possessed of sufficient power to reward his merit and advance him to the highest honors of a free country."

It was everyone's revolution. There was no group in America, large or small, that failed to play some part in the fight for freedom. Immigrants from every nation adopted the cause. Pennsylvania Germans were among the first to join Washington at Boston, later forming an honor guard for the general. Thousands of immigrant Irishmen enlisted in New England units, and new Americans of every other nationality served. The various faiths made their contributions as well, from the Maryland and Massachusetts Catholics to the Huguenots of South Carolina. Even pacifist sects like the Quakers, whose faiths forbade their bearing arms, contributed money and did service as teamsters, physicians, and in other noncombative roles.

Nor was this just a white, Christian revolution. The first Americans, the Indians, saw some duty with the colonists.

Death of Crispus Attucks in "Boston Massacre."

In 1778 Washington was empowered to raise a company of 400 Indians for use as scouts and raiders, and at least one Red man died in winter quarters at Valley Forge after fighting for "his" country. The Indians, particularly the Iroquois, were a major factor in the tenuous Northwest country during the war and though most fought with the British—and paid dearly for it during and after the war—many joined with the colonists in their mutual fight. At the same time, a number of the 2,000 Jews in America during the Revolution made their contribution. Francis Salvador of Charleston, South Carolina died in the first year of the war. In 1777 Mordecai Sheftall became commissary general of purchases and issues for the Georgia Militia. And throughout the war, Haym Salomon helped the fledgling nation finance its way to independence.

Of course, the American Negro, free and slave, played a large part in the Revolution. Peter Salem and other black soldiers fought at Bunker Hill, and Salem himself is credited with killing Major Pitcairn. Though Congress had barred Negroes from enlistment in the Continental Army in

October 1775, Washington ordered that black recruits be accepted, and Congress backed down on the issue. Many white slave holders, under the substitute provisions, sent their slaves into the army in their place, but by far the majority of the blacks who fought were freedmen who did so of their own choosing. In all, about 3,000 served. Over 5 percent of Washington's army at Monmouth were Negro soldiers, and the Continental forces generally averaged about fifty black troops in every battalion. Two of these men, Prince Whipple and Oliver Cromwell, were by Wash-

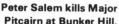

Peter Salem kills Major Pitcairn at Bunker Hill.

ington's side when he crossed the Delaware on Christmas 1776. With the exception of two all-black regiments, one from Rhode Island and one from Massachusetts, Negro soldiers were not segregated in the army. Of course, there was widespread opposition to their service, predominately from the Northern slave traders and Southern plantation owners, but the blacks proved themselves in battle. A few, like Edward Griffin of North Carolina, were freed by state

Molly Pitcher at the Battle of Monmouth.

edict in return for their services. In one battle alone, during the withdrawal of Sullivan from Newport, the newly formed black regiment from Rhode Island, 400 strong, withstood three "furious assaults" by some 1,500 Hessians.

While the men were fighting, the women of the Revolution cooked, nursed, ran hospitals, sewed, raised supplies and money, and suffered hardship and privation for the cause. Many followed their husbands in the army, making life in war a little more tolerable by preparing meals for soldiers. Others spent their time within sight and sound of the enemy, spying and carrying information back to the rebels. They melted their pewter into bullets, and made their bedding into clothing. Mrs. David Wright of Groton, Massachusetts was elected sergeant of a company of soldiers' wives who banded together after their husbands went off to war. These "minutewomen" captured at least one Tory, and provided information to Continental authorities. And, of course, there were the numerous "Molly Pitchers" of real and legendary fame, like Mary Hays, who manned a cannon at Monmouth, and Molly Corbin, who took her dying husband's place at a gun in the defense of Fort Washington. Whatever their mode of service, the women of Colonial America did their part and more for the winning of independence.

Mrs. Philip Schuyler setting grain fields on fire to thwart British invaders.

Major General Israel Putnam, commander at Heights of Guan.

Major General John Sullivan, inept subordinate to Putnam.

The
Fight for
New York

*W*ashington realized that the key to the defense of Manhattan lay beyond the limits of the island. Directly across the East River was Long Island, the village of Brooklyn, and more important, Brooklyn Heights, which rose a hundred feet above the river, a situation very similar to Dorchester Heights and Boston. Whoever occupied Brooklyn Heights would control the river and most of New York. Here Washington had a series of forts and strong earthworks constructed. About a mile and a half south of these fortifications was another ridge of hills called the Heights of Guan, which formed a natural barrier protecting the defenses on Brooklyn Heights. General Putnam, in command, placed about 3,000 of his 10,000 men along this line under the immediate command of General John Sullivan, a mediocre officer. Putnam knew practically nothing about the topography of the island, and as a result his disposition of troops was extremely faulty.

By late August Howe was ready to move. From the 22d to the 25th he landed about 22,000 troops unopposed at Gravesend on the tip of Long Island. Then under cover of darkness the night of the 26th he moved the bulk of his force in an all-night march around the left flank of the American advance line, leaving the rest to demonstrate against the American center and right. At the same time he ordered Admiral Howe to sail his warships up the river to bombard the Brooklyn fortifications and cut off a possible retreat route for the rebels. The move caught the Americans completely by surprise, and by noon the next day Howe had swept the ridge clear of all rebels, who fled in panic back to the fortifications at Brooklyn, suffering about 1,500 casualties to the Britishers' 377. Fortunately for the American cause, a stiff north wind and a swift ebbing tide prevented Admiral Howe from sailing his flotilla of warships up the East River to within supporting distance of the land forces. Had he succeeded, it is entirely possible that the whole American army might have been killed or captured, and the revolution brought to an end right there.

Admiral Sir Richard Howe, British fleet commander.

American General Lord Stirling at the Battle of Long Island.

By late afternoon all who escaped death or capture were safely within the fortified lines on Brooklyn Heights. Washington, who had been on the field since early morning, now sent to New York for reinforcements. Anxiously the disheartened Americans waited for the expected concentrated attack, but it never came. Instead Howe drew back and halted, then began preparations for a regular siege approach, to the utter consternation of many of his officers. Howe, apparently, was still scarred by the memory of Bunker Hill. One of his officers recorded in his journal the bitterness and frustration many of them felt at this critical failure to continue the attack. "Far from taking the rash resolution of hastily passing over the East River . . . and crushing at once a frightened, trembling enemy, he generously gave them time to recover from their panic,—to throw up fresh works,—to make new arrangements,—and to recover from the torpid state the rebellion appeared in from its late shock."

All the next day Howe still did not move. That afternoon a cold northeaster blew up and pelted the hapless and

Old engraving shows Washington's retreat from Long Island.

Brigadier General John Glover's fishermen moved the American Army off Long Island.

hungry Americans. "We had no tents to screen us from its pitiless pelting," wrote an officer. For food all they had was hard biscuits and pickled pork, eaten raw because fires were impossible in the downpour. Despite their suffering, however, nature really helped the rebels, for the storm kept the British fleet out of the East River and left an avenue of retreat open if needed.

Finally realizing his precarious position, on the morning of the 29th Washington ordered his officers in New York to gather all boats fit for transporting troops and to assemble them by dark. The handling of these boats was entrusted to Colonel John Glover's regiment of Marblehead, Massachusetts fishermen. During the night the retreat began. A Connecticut major described what happened:

> To move so large a body of troops with all their necessary appendages across a river full a mile wide, with a rapid current, in face of a victorious, well-disciplined army nearly three times as numerous as his own and a fleet capable of stopping the navigation so that not one boat could have passed over, seemed to present most formidable obstacles. But in the face of these difficulties, the Commander in Chief so arranged his business that on the evening of the twenty-ninth by ten o'clock, the troops began to retire from the lines in such a manner that no chasm was made in the lines, but as one regiment left their station on guard, the remaining troops moved to the right and left and filled up the vacancies, while Gen. Washington took his station at the ferry and superintended the embarkation of the troops. It was one of the most anxious, busy nights I ever recollect; and being the third in which hardly any of us had closed our eyes in sleep, we were all greatly fatigued.

In the face of complete disaster, Washington succeeded in extricating 9,500 men with all their supplies and equipment from under Howe's very nose. The noted English historian Trevelyan stated it was "a master stroke of energy, dexterity, and caution, by which Washington saved his army and his country."

This brilliant stroke was undoubtedly crucial to the Patriot cause, as after the defeat on the 27th and the chance of complete annihilation the morale of the Americans had been shattered. One officer observed, "if independence had not been declared before the battle of the 27th, it is the opinion of the writer that it would not have been declared." That was apparently Howe's belief also, because instead of vigorously pursuing Washington he now delayed several vital weeks while he sent General Sullivan, who had been captured, to Congress to suggest an informal peace conference to discuss reconciliation. Benjamin Franklin, John Adams, and Edmund Rutledge were appointed to meet with Howe. The conference was held on Staten Island September 11, but when Howe insisted that revocation of the Resolution of Independence was a necessary prelude to any peace negotiations, the meeting broke up. Had independence not been declared, it is highly probable that the rebellion would have ended then and there.

Interview between Admiral Lord Howe and American Council, by John Ward Dunsmore. *(Courtesy The Title Guarantee Co.)*

After the failure of the peace conference Washington, realizing that the British occupation of Brooklyn Heights made his position on lower Manhattan untenable, immediately started a withdrawal to a new line on Harlem Heights. For a change Howe reacted quickly and almost succeeded in capturing a large part of the American army with a surprise landing at Kip's Bay on the rebel left flank September 15. But the withdrawal continued, and Washington succeeded in consolidating his forces on the strong natural defensive terrain of the Heights, where he established a three-line defense in depth. The next day the British advance party made a weak attack which was

Battle of Harlem Heights. *("Harper's Weekly," Sept. 30, 1876)*

quickly repulsed, while the rebels continued to erect strong entrenchments.

Again Howe had no stomach for attacking the rebels behind fortifications. Instead, he planned once more to outflank them. During the night of October 12 he embarked the bulk of his army, sailed up the East River and Long Island Sound, and landed at Pell's Point in Westchester. This move imperiled the American army. Consequently, Washington moved to White Plains, leaving strong garrisons under General Nathanael Greene in Fort Washington and Fort Lee across the river on the Palisades in New Jersey. The rebels formed a three-mile-wide line through the village of White Plains, but unfortunately neglected to fortify a strategic elevation on their right. When Howe attacked October 28 and seized the hill, Washington was forced to withdraw to a new position five miles north at North Castle.

The Continentals. Drawing by Howard Pyle.

The Perilous

CARLTON CHAPMAN.

While Washington was thus engaged in striving to keep his little army intact, another threat developed on the American northern front. After driving the rebels out of Canada, Carleton had been reinforced to about 13,000 including German mercenaries and Indians, but he was not ready to

Winter

**Major General
Benedict Arnold,
American leader at
Valcour Bay.**

**Battle of Valcour Bay.
*("Scribner's Magazine,"
Feb. 1898)***

move south until September. The key to his success was control of Lake Champlain, which both he and Arnold, in command of naval operations on the lake, realized. While Carleton was building and assembling gunboats and sailing vessels, Arnold, who knew something about boats from his

British fleet forcing the Hudson River
passage. U.S. Navy photo of Dominique Serres painting.

experiences as a West Indies trader, succeeded under almost impossible conditions in getting about fifteen ships of various types built and manned by motley crews, most of them inexperienced. October 11-13 the two forces met at Valcour Bay, and Carleton's experienced sailors and superior equipment swept the little American flotilla from the lake. But the delay this caused Carleton was decisive. He concluded he was now not prepared for a winter campaign

General George Washington
at Princeton, by Charles
Willson Peale. (*Courtesy of
The Pennsylvania Academy
of the Fine Arts*)

and, instead of laying siege to Fort Ticonderoga and coming down the Hudson to join Howe, he retreated back into Canada for the winter, an action which undoubtedly helped save the American cause.

Howe now changed his tactics. Instead of pursuing the main American force, he turned south and on November 16 attacked isolated Fort Washington with about 8,000 men. Although Washington had advised Greene to evacuate the fort, Greene, as yet inexperienced, chose to keep the gar-

"Washington Crossing the Delaware," by Emanuel Leutz.
(The Metropolitan Museum of Art, Gift of John S. Kennedy, 1897.)

rison there, and when it was forced to surrender the Americans lost over 2,800 men, most of them captured, while the British suffered only about 450 casualties. Then Cornwallis led a force of 6,000 across the Hudson, mounted artillery on the Palisades, and forced Greene to evacuate Fort Lee with the loss of desperately needed supplies.

Greene and Washington then joined forces at Hackensack

and retreated across New Jersey toward the Delaware River, with Cornwallis close on their heels. On December 7 the rebels crossed the river into Pennsylvania, seizing or destroying all the boats they could find. After his unsuccessful chase, Cornwallis stopped at the Delaware as the British advance bogged down. "As we go forward into the country the rebels fly before us," a British officer noted, "and when we come back they always follow us. 'Tis almost impossible to catch them. They will neither fight, nor totally run away, but they keep at such a distance that we are always a day's march from them." Howe then declared his campaign at an end for the winter and sent the bulk of his force back to New York, leaving garrisons at Trenton, Princeton, and Bordentown, with a supply base at New Brunswick.

It seemed as winter approached after a year and a half of war that Washington had achieved his big objective, the preservation of his army. So long as Washington and that army existed, the rebellion would go on regardless of what territory the British might control. But in fact the army was on the verge of collapse. Desertions, disease, lack of supplies, and apathy on the part of the Congress and the people of the colonies threatened to destroy it. Wrote Washington: "The conduct of the Jerseys has been most infamous. Instead of turning out to defend their country, and affording aid to our army, they are making their submissions as fast as they can. If they had given us any support, we might have made a stand at Hackensack and after that at Brunswick, but the few militia that were in arms, disbanded themselves . . . and left the poor remains of our army to make the best we could of it." A British general wrote to the commander of the Hessian garrison at Trenton that the American army was "almost naked, dying of cold, without blankets, and very ill-supplied with provisions." It was that December that Thomas Paine, the propagandist of the Revolution,

The Battle of Trenton. *("Harper's Encyclopedia of United States History")*

wrote his famous words: "These are the times that try men's souls. The summer soldier and the sunshine patriot will, in this crisis, shrink from the service of their country; but he that stands it *now* deserves the love and thanks of man and woman."

Washington realized in desperation that something had to be done, and done quickly, to restore morale and arouse interest in the cause of freedom. He decided on a surprise attack on the ill-prepared force at Trenton. Christmas night he led about 2,400 men across the ice-choked Delaware in a blinding snow and sleet storm, and early the next morning attacked the sleeping Hessians in two columns. The surprise was complete. In less than an hour almost 1,000 Hessians were captured or killed, while the rebels suffered only five casualties. The Patriot cause now took on new hope and enlistments started to pick up. An American officer observed, "Never were men in higher spirits than our whole army is."

Howe reacted quickly to this embarrassing defeat. He ordered Cornwallis into Jersey with heavy reinforcements to crush the small rebel force. Cornwallis reached Trenton January 2 but then rejected the advice of his officers to attack at once, stating that he could just as well "bag the fox" the next morning, to which one of his officers replied, "My Lord, if you trust those people tonight, you will see nothing of them in the morning." Leaving his campfires burning and just enough men to give the appearance of an occupied camp, Washington stole around Cornwallis' flank and by dawn was close to Princeton, where he routed a British force coming up to join his antagonist. Hearing the sound of battle in his rear, Cornwallis fell back to Brunswick to protect his supply base, and Washington led his exhausted troops into winter quarters in the hills around Morristown.

The Battle of Princeton. Engraving from painting by Alonzo Chappel.

Some regulars of the Continental Army. Note ox-drawn cannon.

With these two quick victories, Washington had cleared all but eastern New Jersey of British troops, but more important he had restored the shattered morale of the Americans. A British civilian noted that now "volunteer companies are collecting in every county on the continent and in a few months the rascals will be stronger than ever. Even the parsons, some of them, have turned out as volunteers and pulpit drums or thunder, which you please to call it, summoning all to arms in this cursed bobble. Damn them all."

Although these volunteers and the state militia were a vital element—indeed the war could not have been won without them—it was almost impossible for Washington to make any long range plans concerning them. Most of the volunteers came to fight one or two battles near their homes and then disappeared again. In too many cases the state militia were little better. Prior to 1775 nearly every able-bodied man between 16 and 50 served in the militia, organized primarily for defense against the Indians, and in some places the French. Most of the time, however, it was more a social club than a military organization. Usually the enlisted men elected their officers and disposed of them in like manner. Strict military discipline was practically unknown. Oftentimes their enlistment was for three, six, or nine months, and when their term expired they promptly took off for home regardless of the military situation or the wishes of their officers. Consequently, they could not be consistently relied upon.

British drawing of
American officer.
(A.S.K. Brown
Military Collection)

German drawing of
American soldier.
(A.S.K. Brown
Military Collection)

The men Washington had to rely on, in fact the very nucleus of the war as it was fought, were the Regulars of the Continental Army. Although possibly as many as 300,000 served at one time or another during the war, out of a total population of about 3 million, there were probably not more than 17,000 Regulars all told. In 1776 the Continental Congress changed the oath of enlistment for the Regulars from one to three years or the duration of the war. As an inducement for the extra service a bounty of $10 (later raised to $20 and 100 acres of land) was paid, but the basic pay remained the same, $6 2/3 a month. The fact that this was probably the highest pay soldiers had ever received in any war was little consolation to the man who had to pay $100 for a good pair of boots and $6 for a quart of poor whiskey. By 1780 a laborer's pay for a day equalled what the soldier received for a month. Not that it mattered particularly, because the soldier seldom got paid anyway. On the rare occasions when he did, with characteristic military humor he called it his "three drunks" and let it go at that. He noted with some bitterness, however, that wherever the army went prices increased accordingly. Sometimes he supplied his own clothing, for which he was allowed $20, although he was supposed to be issued "one suit" of brown or gray a year and charged $1.67 per month until it was paid for. It wasn't until 1782 that Congress decreed all uniforms should be blue, faced with red, lined with white, and with white buttons. The most common uniform, if indeed it could

German drawing of Pennsylvania riflemen. *(A.S.K. Brown Military Collection)*

One of Morgan's riflemen.

be called that, was the long brown or gray hunting shirt, buckskin breeches, and a round hat with the brim sometimes turned up in three places. He was also entitled to a daily ration of one pound of fresh beef or salt fish, or three-quarters of a pound of pork, one pound of bread or flour, one pint of milk, one quart of spruce beer or cider; and a weekly allowance of peas, beans, or other vegetables, along with rice, molasses, candles, soap, and vinegar. On the march or in the field he was allowed one pound of beef or pork and one pound of hard bread. In cold or wet weather, on guard duty or fatigue detail, he was entitled to a gill of rum or whiskey, when and if it was available. As any schoolchild knows, this was mere wishful thinking by Congress. At no time during the war did the Continental Army ever present a "uniform" appearance, and the diaries, letters, and journals of the period abound with references to the starving condition of the soldiers, particularly in the winter months.

It was a time when men died as quickly from their cures as from their ills. The *materia medica* consisted of mercury, quinine, antimony, Peruvian bark, jalop, ipecac, spirits of ammonia, salts of tartar, calomel, and sulphur; therapy was primarily bloodletting, blistering, purgatives, and emetics; and doctors were without antiseptics or anesthesia. Few

British "Brown Bess."

specific remedies were known, and because of inadequate knowledge of sanitation, smallpox, typhus, tuberculosis, typhoid, venereal disease, pleurisy, and dysentery raged almost uncontrolled throughout the camps. Dr. Benjamin Rush, when Surgeon General of the Continental Army, sadly admitted that disease and hospitals "robbed the United States of more citizens than the sword." In 1776 it was estimated that 1,000 rebels were killed in combat and 1,200 wounded, while about 10,000 died from sickness and disease.

Regardless of the hard living and dying, however, the American soldier could still play when the opportunity presented itself. Despite Washington's order against all "gaming," dice and cards were popular pastimes, along with marksmanship contests, bowling, foot races, wrestling, swimming, hunting, fishing, and singing. But as with all armies from time immemorial, liquor and women were probably the most popular forms of recreation. It was not unusual for wives and washerwomen to accompany the troops, but the majority of the women following the army, "these bitchfoxly jades, jills, hags, prostitutes," as one officer called them, were plying an older profession and caused much trouble. Baggage and knapsacks were continually stolen on the frequent moves, and "a great many have lost their clothes by the whores and rogues that went with the baggage."

American rifle.

Detail of lock, iron-mounted rifle.

Victory, Defeats,

By spring of 1777 the Patriot army was up to over 10,000 men and in relatively good condition. Then Howe surprised Washington by withdrawing all his troops to New York, with the exception of a small force at Amboy. During the winter the British ministry had approved a new plan for conquering New York and isolating the New England states. A strong force commanded by General John Burgoyne would push down Lake Champlain and the

and Valley Forge

General "Gentleman Johnny" Burgoyne, conquered at Saratoga.

General Burgoyne addressing his Indian allies.

Hudson River; a secondary force consisting primarily of Loyalists and Indians would operate from Oswego through the Mohawk Valley; and a large detachment from Howe's army would move up the Hudson and join Burgoyne at Albany. This was an excellent plan, but the ministry also approved at the same time Howe's plan to capture Philadelphia, in the mistaken belief that he could accomplish that and still join Burgoyne in time.

On June 17 Burgoyne moved south from Canada with a force of 9,400, including British and German troops, Canadians, Loyalists, and Indians. July 6 he captured Fort Ticonderoga and substantial American supplies. Moving on quickly, Burgoyne continued his advance south, but then things began to go wrong for the British. Rough terrain and the delaying tactics of General Philip John Schuyler's troops, who felled trees, destroyed bridges, and burned

Hessian captured by militiaman.

84

crops, slowed his progress and strained his supplies. The secondary force coming through the Mohawk Valley

The Battle of Bennington, from painting by Alonzo Chappel.

stopped to besiege Fort Stanwix, but when they learned that Arnold with a force of about 1,000 was coming to the fort's support they retreated back into Canada. To make matters worse, Howe was not coming from New York. On July 23 he set sail for Philadelphia with 15,000 troops, leaving Clinton to hold New York with a small force.

By early August Burgoyne's supply situation was critical. Learning of a large store of American supplies at Bennington, Vermont, he sent a detachment of about 800 to seize it. But an aroused band of New England militia,

**General Horatio Gates,
victor at Saratoga.** *(Bryant's
"Popular History of the
United States")*

alarmed by stories of Indian atrocities, routed this force as
well as reinforcements sent later on August 16, inflicting
about 1,000 casualties. Burgoyne now had a crucial decision
to make. Retreat to Canada or gamble and push on toward
Albany. He chose the latter.

September 13 the British crossed to the west bank of the
Hudson and four miles north of the village of Stillwater they
came upon the Americans, about 9,000 men commanded by
General Horatio Gates, entrenched in a strong position on

Wounding of Arnold at Saratoga.

Gates receives Burgoyne's surrender. At left are Schuyler and Morgan. *(From painting by H. A. Ogden)*

Bemis Heights, where the road to Albany passed through a narrow defile. The American position commanded both the road and the river. On September 19 Burgoyne attacked the rebel left in an attempt to gain some high ground, but was checked short of his objective after a furious, day-long fight. The British commander then decided to entrench and await help from Clinton in New York. And for three weeks he waited in vain. Clinton did move up the Hudson and on October 6 captured some forts below Albany, but then decided he needed reinforcements before advancing farther and retreated back to New York, leaving Burgoyne isolated.

Realizing his situation was desperate, Burgoyne tried once more on October 7 to cave in the American left, but when that failed he retreated northward to the heights around Saratoga. But there an American force that had now grown to about 20,000 surrounded his hungry troops. On October 17 he surrendered his entire army, consisting now of only about 6,000 men. This British disaster proved to be the turning point of the war. When news of the American

Battle of the Brandywine, by F. C. Yohn. ("Scribner's Magazine," June 1898)

victory reached Europe, France decided to aid the Americans openly by recognizing their independence, entering into a treaty of amity and commerce, and agreeing to a treaty of alliance if and when war broke out between Britain and France. This was the aid and support the Americans had to have in order to achieve independence.

Washington, meanwhile, had not fared so well. After finally leaving New York in July, Howe, instead of proceeding directly up the Delaware to Philadelphia, sailed up Chesapeake Bay and on August 25 landed at Head of Elk, fifty-five miles from the city. Washington, with about 11,000 troops, took up a defensive position to block him on the east side of Brandywine Creek. Howe attacked

September 11 using a flanking movement similar to that employed in the Battle of Long Island. Washington was routed and forced to withdraw across the Schuylkill River, suffering over 1,000 casualties to about half that number for the British. Congress fled to Lancaster, and later to York, as the British occupied Philadelphia, with their main encampment at Germantown.

Washington now planned a surprise attack against Howe at his base in Germantown with a series of complicated maneuvers requiring almost perfect coordination and timing. Under cover of a heavy fog before dawn on the morning of October 4 he threw two columns at the British center,

Battle of Germantown: attack on the Chew House.

while another two columns were ordered to attack both flanks simultaneously. Unfortunately, the British were not taken completely by surprise, and when the necessary co-ordination did not take place, the attack slowed. Then some American troops, confused in the fog, fired on each other and the rumor started that the British were in their rear. Panic set in and the attack turned into a disorderly retreat. The Americans suffered over 700 casualties.

Despite these two defeats and the loss of Philadelphia, morale was surprisingly high as Washington in December led his battered army into winter quarters at Valley Forge on the banks of the Schuylkill. Undoubtedly the great victory at Saratoga helped. But Washington was to learn that winter encampments for the Continental Army could be even more trying and costly than battles in the field. He had selected these desolate winter quarters for a definite purpose—to protect the citizens of Pennsylvania and New Jersey from the marauding enemy, and at the same time to guard the main road from the south to New England. For this he was severely criticized by the very people he was trying to protect, many of his officers, and members of Congress. He told them: "My answer is that our hopes are not placed in any particular city or spot of ground, but in preserving a good army, furnished with proper necessaries, to take advantage of favorable opportunities, and master and defeat the enemy piecemeal."

But when they arrived at Valley Forge Washington discovered that Congress and the quartermaster-general

The winter at Valley Forge. By Alonzo Chappel.

View of Philadelphia, showing Christ Church. *(Independence National Historical Park)*

91

had failed to secure and transport the necessary supplies, and the local farmers, mostly Loyalist in sympathy, were unwilling to sell their produce to the rebels. There was fresh pork aplenty in New Jersey and barrels of flour along the Susquehanna, but the wagons and horses needed to transport these supplies were lacking. A crueler hurt was the knowledge that there was ample flour and wheat in New York being sold to civilians and the British; that the farmers in Connecticut refused to sell meat to the army because of a price ceiling put on it by Congress; and that Boston merchants would not do business with Congress except for exorbitant profits, and then only for hard cash, not Continental paper. Thus Washington was forced to witness the terrible, tragic sight of his soldiers literally starving and freezing to death in a land of plenty. He wrote to Congress: "I am now convinced that unless some great and capital change suddenly takes place, this Army must inevitably be reduced to one or other of these three things: starve, dissolve, or disperse in order to obtain subsistence in the best manner they can."

Why didn't the army dissolve or disperse? Was it because the men could humorously remark that for supper many nights they ate "a leg of nothing and no turnups"; or that "soldiers live sometimes better but never worse." Was it, perhaps, the feeling that "the man who has seen misery knows best how to enjoy good." Or was it the belief that "Providence will find out a way for my relief." The answer is not easy to find. It had something to do with what we casually call the "Spirit of 'Seventy-six." There was something in the air—a feeling, a spirit, a belief, call it what you will—it was there and it tugged at the imagination.

But before the hellish winter was over 2,500 men had died and more than 2,000 deserted or refused to enlist when their terms expired, until the 11,000 Washington had led into camp numbered fewer than 6,000, and at one period almost

3,000 of these were unfit for duty owing to lack of shoes and clothing. Yet the Pennsylvania legislature had the arrogance to pass a resolution severely censuring Washington for not attacking the British forces comfortably housed and well supplied in Philadelphia!

So they suffered and existed somehow, held together by the magnetism of their general and their cause, through the winter they had to fight harder than they would ever have to fight the enemy. When the snow in the passes melted in the early spring, the food wagons began to trickle in and the plentiful shad came up the river to spawn. A foreign officer, calling himself Baron von Steuben, came to teach them to drill and march and maneuver efficiently, to use their bayonets to best advantage; and he discovered the hidden

Major General Baron Von Steuben, by Ralph Earl. (New York Historical Ass'n., Cooperstown, N.Y.)

power, fortitude, and originality that existed there. "The genius of this nation," he wrote, "is not in the least to be compared with that of the Prussians, Austrians or French. You say to your soldier 'Do this' and he doeth it, but I am obliged to say 'This is the reason why you ought to do that,' and then he does it." Thus by late spring the army under Washington's leadership came out of Valley Forge a better trained and disciplined fighting force than before.

Battle of Monmouth, by H. Ditzlar.
("Scribner's Magazine," June 1898)

John Paul Jones, from painting by Charles Willson Peale.

The
Sea War

*H*owe had missed a wonderful opportunity to destroy the Americans. He had made no move all winter to attack the rebels, critically short of food and supplies, although they were only twenty miles from Philadelphia. In May he was relieved and replaced by Clinton. But Clinton brought orders for the evacuation of Philadelphia, much to the disgust of the local Loyalists. With the advent of the French Alliance and the threat of the French Navy, the British did not want to keep their lines extended so far. So in June they moved out across New Jersey on the way back to New York. Washington followed, sending a strong force under General Charles Lee ahead to strike Clinton's extended column. Lee attacked June 28 at Monmouth Courthouse, but badly bungled the affair. Washington arrived just in time to stop a complete rout and succeeded in beating back the British counterattack. Clinton stole away that night and retreated safely to New York. Washington then took up a position at White Plains, just above New York, and waited to see what Clinton would do next.

Meanwhile, France and England had declared war, and a French fleet under the Comte d'Estaing with 4,000 troops was sent to support the Americans. Arriving off New York in July, it did not attack the British there because the French ships were too big to maneuver in the narrow channel. Instead, a joint operation against the British garrison of 3,000 at Newport, Rhode Island was planned. D'Estaing would attack from the sea, while an American force under General Sullivan would invest the British from the land side. The French arrived July 29 but Sullivan was not ready as he had difficulty raising the necessary number of militia. By the time he was ready Clinton had sent Admiral Howe's fleet to the aid of the besieged force. D'Estaing backed off to prepare for a decisive naval battle with Howe, but a fierce storm on August 11 scattered both fleets. The French then repaired their ships at Boston and sailed for the West Indies. Sullivan, without naval support, was forced to withdraw.

Strictly speaking, from the colonial standpoint, there was no naval war during the Revolution. While several colonies maintained their own sea forces, America did not put a real navy at sea during the conflict but, instead, made her influence felt on the sea lanes by an energetic, and highly effective, privateering fleet. Estimates of the number of American ships given letters of marque for privateering range as high as 2,000, the great majority of them commissioned by Congress. In the eight years of the war, they captured some 600 enemy ships, taking an estimated $18,000,000 worth of property. One privateer alone, the *Rattlesnake*, captured ships and cargoes totaling $1,000,000 in a single cruise in the Baltic. In 1781, there were some 449 privateers actively engaged in combing the oceans for British shipping. Unfortunately, since the captured ships were sold in foreign ports, and the officers and crews of the privateers divided the money and proceeds from sale of cargoes, the American cause realized little from the program other than its nuisance value to the British and the morale uplift for the colonists at home.

The real Continental Navy, such as it was, posed no threat to British naval might. There had been minor naval actions at Machias, Maine in May 1775, and during the siege of Boston, but the colonists did not actually commission a war vessel until Washington sent the *Hannah* to harass enemy supply on September 2, 1775. One month later Congress commissioned four warships. The Marines were given birth in November, and on the 25th the Navy

The French fleet sailing toward Boston, by Pierre Ozanne. ("Fraternité D'Armes Franco-Américaine")

was finally established officially. Eight vessels were constructed, including the *Hornet, Wasp,* and *Fly,* and captains commissioned. Esek Hopkins was named commander in chief, and the ranking lieutenant was John Paul Jones. Hopkins' first, and only, fleet action was the capture of Nassau, Bahamas in March 1776. After that, Jones took the spotlight and held it for the rest of the year by capturing or sinking twenty-two enemy vessels.

The "Bonhomme Richard" and the "Serapis." Drawn by E. C. Peixotto.

Captain John Barry.

The French alliance brought a new fleet to the American coast, but it enjoyed only frustration until 1781. Meanwhile, John Paul Jones continued to plague the British in his ship *Ranger,* actually raiding Whitehaven, England in April 1778, and later winning a militarily unimportant, but spectacular and much publicized, victory on September 23, 1779 when his new command, *Bonhomme Richard,* met and defeated the *Serapis.* There were a number of other equally glamorous encounters, particularly those of the intrepid Captain James Nicholson of the *Trumbull,* and Captain John Barry's *Alliance,* which fought the last real naval battle of the war in January 1783. However, none of these engagements had a very significant military impact on the war's outcome. By and large, the naval war was a sideshow while the real issue was decided on land. Nevertheless, her victories at sea went far toward maintaining America's spirit when the armies were retreating and, as well, they formed the basis of American naval tradition for the time when the United States would be one of the great sea powers of the world.

**Surrender of Vincennes. Hamilton tenders his sword to Clark.
Painted by F. C. Yohn.** *(Courtesy Indiana Historical Bureau)*

Uncertain Years 1778-80

*F*or all intents and purposes, the war in the north was now over. Washington later conducted a series of raids on British-held forts and an expedition was sent against the Indians and Loyalists in western Pennsylvania and New York, but no major actions took place.

An almost separate war, however, was taking place about this time in what was then called the Northwest. Most of the colonies had claims to the lands west of the Appalachians, but none of these were as extensive or as valid as Virginia's. Even as the Revolution was being fought settlers had been travelling over the Wilderness Road into Kentucky and Tennessee, but the British with strong posts at Detroit and Niagara had organized the Indians, enabling them to control the area and to harass the frontier settlers.

In December 1777, Governor Patrick Henry of Virginia met with Colonel George Rogers Clark and proposed that the latter command an expedition against the lightly held British posts in the Northwest, then claimed by Virginia. The following May, Clark left Redstone Fort, Pennsylvania with some 200 men, and floated down the Ohio on his way to the first objective, British-held Kaskaskia on the Mississippi. Clark invested the village on the night of July 4, and the next day the British surrendered to the Americans without the loss of a life. Nearby Cahokia capitulated next.

George Rogers Clark

The French inhabitants of the region, upon learning from Clark of the French Alliance, embraced the American cause, and through the efforts of the French priest, Father Gibault, the villagers of Vincennes pledged an oath to the new American flag.

Lieutenant Governor Henry Hamilton, in Detroit, upon hearing that Clark had wrested the Northwest from British control, prepared to regain the territory. On December 17, 1778 Hamilton, with a force of 500 British and Indians, descended upon Vincennes and recaptured the fort (Fort Sackville) and village. Word of Hamilton's sudden appearance at Vincennes reached Clark at Kaskaskia at a time when his forces were dangerously reduced by the expiration of enlistments. However, Clark soon learned that Hamilton, feeling secure for the winter at Fort Sackville, had reduced his own forces to only eighty men. Gathering 170 men, including French volunteers from the nearby settlements, Clark began his famous march (February 5, 1779) against Vincennes in heavy rains and across the flooded lands of the Wabash. Wading through icy water often breast high, Clark's little army reached Vincennes on February 24, 1779 and opened a deadly fire upon the gun ports of Fort Sackville, preventing the surprised British gunners from manning their pieces. The following day, Hamilton surrendered the post. Through Clark's brilliant maneuverings the Northwest had been secured and British power in the region driven back to Detroit.

Unable to mount a successful drive from Canada, and having failed in their efforts to take and hold the Middle Colonies, the British decided that a final attempt to crush the rebellion would be made in the Southern Colonies. This decision was influenced by the belief that a large number of Loyalists would aid them, particularly in the Carolinas. As the first step in this operation Clinton dispatched a force of about 3,500 from New York to Savannah, Georgia. On December 29, 1778 Savannah fell, and shortly thereafter the British captured Augusta. Then they conducted a series of raids up and down the coast from Charleston to Florida. In the spring Washington sent a detachment of Continental Regulars under General Benjamin Lincoln to try to recapture Augusta, but Lincoln was defeated. The British at last seemed to be on the way to some significant success.

But then in June 1779 Spain declared war on England, and in September d'Estaing arrived off Savannah with thirty-five ships and 4,000 French troops. Lincoln with

Lieutenant General
Comte d'Estaing.
("Fraternité D'Armes
Franco-Américaine")

1,400 men joined the French and they besieged the city but
d'Estaing was impatient, and on October 9 ordered an assault on the strong British fortifications. The attack failed,
the Americans suffered over 800 casualties, and d'Estaing
was wounded. He then sailed again to the West Indies.
Heartened by this, Clinton now decided to use a major force

Attack on Savannah, October 8, 1779. *("Scribner's," 1898)*

to conquer the South, using Savannah as his base. He evacuated the garrison from Rhode Island and on December 26 sailed from New York with over 8,000 troops, leaving about 10,000 in New York to keep Washington from making a countermove. The objective once again was Charleston, South Carolina.

In December Washington again moved his army of about 11,000 into winter quarters near Morristown, New Jersey. Even as the men set to work chopping down trees to build their crude log huts, the weather turned bitterly cold and one snowstorm after another howled through the area. Again Congress did not send the needed supplies and the men "suffered much without shoes and stockings and working half leg deep in snow." It turned out to be the worst winter of the war and the troops suffered much more than they had at Valley Forge two years earlier. A terrible storm in January left almost four feet of snow on the ground, and as one officer observed, "the sufferings of the poor soldiers can scarcely be described. While on duty they are unavoidably exposed to all the inclemency of storms and severe cold. At night they now have a bed of straw on the ground and a single blanket to each man. They are badly clad and some are destitute of shoes." When the snows blocked the roads and wagons couldn't move, the army again was in danger of starving. One soldier recorded in his journal: "I do solemnly declare that I did not put a single morsel of victuals into my mouth for four days and as many nights, except a little black birch bark, which I knawed off a stick of wood, if that can be called victuals." Realizing that

Washington's headquarters, the Ford Mansion at Morristown. *(National Park Service photo)*

Siege of Charleston. From painting by Alonzo Chappel.

no help could be expected from normal channels, Washington appealed to the local population for help, which was cheerfully and generously given. This alone saved the army from starvation and disbandment.

Spring finally brought some relief, at least from the weather, but it also brought bad news from the South. Clinton had arrived off the Carolina coast in February and had little trouble entering Charleston harbor. The forts on Sullivan's and James Islands had been allowed to fall into disrepair and were no longer tenable, and there was no artillery defense against an attacking fleet. Lincoln then made the fatal error of committing his whole force inside the city, and by early April Clinton completed its investment. Unable to break out of the siege, Lincoln surrendered his entire force of about 5,000, including almost 2,000 Continentals. This was the greatest loss the Americans suffered during the entire war. Leaving Cornwallis to carry on the campaign, Clinton sailed back to New York satisfied that South Carolina was securely in British control.

In May Washington almost had a mutiny on his hands. Two Connecticut regiments, tired of their pay being in arrears, and having been without meat or decent food for several days, ignored their officers and demonstrated on the parade ground until they were disarmed by Pennsylvania troops. No violence occurred and most of the men were pardoned, but it was a clear warning of what could happen if things did not improve.

The year had started badly for the Americans, but that summer a new ray of hope appeared. In July a new French force of 5,000 under the command of the Comte de Rochambeau with a naval escort arrived at Newport, Rhode Island. Washington was now hopeful that a combined attack could be made on New York, but Howe

Comte de Rochambeau.
("Fraternité D'Armes Franco-Américaine")

The American defeat at Camden.

immediately sent a British fleet to blockade Newport. Without the necessary naval support, Washington had to abandon the idea. Still the American forces were gradually growing stronger, more help was expected from the French, and if the British could be contained in the South then the cause of freedom was still healthy.

Congress appointed General Gates, the hero of Saratoga, to lead the attempt to contain the British in the South, although Washington had recommended Greene. Gates took command in North Carolina in July, of an army of about 4,000, including almost 2,000 Continentals detached from Washington, and started a slow march against the British supply base at Camden, South Carolina. On the morning of August 16 Cornwallis with a force of only about 2,400 surprised the Americans just north of the town. After a series of incredible blunders by Gates, the rebels were completely routed, many throwing away their arms in their panic-stricken flight, derisively called the "Camden races."

Almost half the army was killed or captured, while many of the survivors simply disappeared. Belatedly following Washington's advice, Congress then relieved Gates and appointed Greene to command.

With this defeat of the only large, organized American force in the South, the way was opened for Cornwallis' march north and the invasion of North Carolina. Three parallel forces moved northward in September: Cornwallis with the main force; Colonel Banastre Tarleton commanding the feared British Legion cavalry and light infantry; and Major Patrick Ferguson with 1,100 Tories, all Americans. Ferguson's mission was to protect the western flank of Cornwallis, crush the Patriots in western South Carolina, and rouse the back-country Tories to British support. To the freedom-loving mountain people, Ferguson's mission and command were particularly galling. Not only was his force all Americans, but he was also protecting and recruiting other Tories. So the call went out and soon a band of about 900 mountain yeomen, largely of Scotch-Irish descent, marched against Ferguson and on October 7 killed or captured his entire force at King's Mountain on the border between the Carolinas, suffering fewer than 100 casualties themselves. Thus did a handful of mountain men turn the tide of the war in the South and break the Tory influence in the Carolinas for all time. The victory also halted Cornwallis' advance, forcing him to withdraw back into South Carolina.

The British had once again lost an excellent opportunity to strike a decisive blow against the rebels and, with French aid building up, time was working against them. But Wash-

Battle of King's Mountain, painted by F. C. Yohn.
(National Park Service photo)

ington also had his troubles that winter. On January 1, 1781 about 2,400 Pennsylvania Continentals encamped near Morristown, finally fed up with no pay, food, clothing, or allowances, mutinied against their officers and marched out of camp to present their justified grievances to the Congress in Philadelphia. Fortunately the president of the Pennsylvania Executive Council was able to pacify them with promises of aid, but about half of them left the army anyway. A few weeks later, when several New Jersey regiments mutinied, Washington acted quickly and forcefully. He sent a force of 600 to disarm them and promptly executed two of the leaders.

It was probably fortunate for the American cause that this was the last year of fighting. Yet the fact that the starving, ragged troops held together at all was nothing less than a miracle. It was not that he suffered such privation for the sake of independence that bothered the Continental so much; it was the realization that he literally froze and starved to death in a land of plenty, where profiteers and speculators were reaping fortunes at his expense and luxurious living was commonplace in many parts of the country. When he did rise up in his wrath it was not against the war or independence or even the army; it was against a government, a country, a people who seemed insensible to the hardships, dangers, and privations he suffered. As one veteran explained it, they vented their spleen "at our country and government, then at our officers, and then at ourselves for our imbecility in staying there and starving for an ungrateful people who did not care what became of us."

**Major General
Nathanael Greene**

"The
Destiny
of Millions"

*T*he war in the South was fast coming to a climax. When Greene took command in the Carolinas he wisely realized that he was not strong enough to attack Cornwallis' main force, so he detached about 800 men under General Daniel Morgan to harass the British outposts in western South Carolina, while he tried to rebuild the army that had been shattered at Camden. Cornwallis was not anxious to advance against Greene with a rebel force operating on his western flank, so he sent Tarleton with about 1,100 troops to drive Morgan back against the main British army.

**General Lord
Charles Cornwallis.**

Morgan, his strength now up to about 1,000 Continentals and militia, made a stand at Cowpens (once a cowpasture) on January 17, and in a brilliantly led and executed battle utterly routed the feared Tarleton, killing or capturing almost his entire force, and suffering fewer than 100 casualties himself. More important, however, this dramatic victory over regular British troops, following as it did the decisive defeat of the Loyalists at King's Mountain, raised Patriot morale all over the country. The Southern militia began to turn out in the numbers needed, and reinforcements started to come from the North.

Cornwallis himself now took out after Morgan, but the American eluded him, joined forces with Greene, and retreated across the Dan River into Virginia. Lacking boats and supplies, Cornwallis withdrew into North Carolina. Greene, now with some 4,000 men after getting reinforcements from Virginia, decided to go after Cornwallis, as he outnumbered him about two to one. On March 15 they clashed at Guilford Courthouse in a desperate battle that the Americans almost won until Cornwallis turned his artillery on both British and American troops engaged in hand-to-hand fighting. Greene withdrew, so Cornwallis claimed a victory, but it cost him over 500 casualties, about

25 percent of his force. As one English official stated, "Another such victory would destroy the British army." Too weakened to continue the campaign, Cornwallis retreated to Wilmington, but then decided that the Carolinas could never be secured while Virginia served as a supply and training base, so in April he marched into Virginia. This failure of the British campaign in the Carolinas was based on the fact that the expected Loyalist support never did materialize, due primarily to the American victories at King's Mountain and Cowpens. Cornwallis explained to Clinton: "My present undertaking sits heavy on my mind. I have experienced the distresses and dangers of marching some hundreds of miles, in a country chiefly hostile, without one active or useful friend; without intelligence, and without communication with any part of the country."

Battle of Cowpens—conflict between Colonels Washington and Tarleton. Painting by Alonzo Chappel.

Battle of Guilford Court House by F. C. Yohn. *(Scribner's, 1898)*

Instead of pursuing Cornwallis, Greene decided to leave the defense of Virginia to Washington and marched into South Carolina in an effort to regain control of that state. Although he could claim no victories in a series of engagements during the spring and summer, by fall he had regained control of the area with the lone exception of Charleston.

Cornwallis, meanwhile, had been reinforced in Virginia. Benedict Arnold, the turncoat who had earlier failed in his attempt to betray to the British the fort at West Point, New York, had been appointed to a command in the British army. In January he sacked and burned Richmond and now joined forces with Cornwallis. With additional reinforcements under General Phillips, Cornwallis had over 7,000

Marie Joseph Paul Ives Roch Gilbert du Motier, Marquis de Lafayette. *(Bryant's "Popular History of the United States")*

men and raided freely throughout Virginia. Von Steuben, in command of the Virginia forces, was hopelessly outnumbered. Washington sent the Marquis de Lafayette with three regiments to von Steuben's support, and in the face of this Cornwallis decided to establish a base on the coast from which he could maintain communication with Clinton in New York. On August 1 he arrived in Yorktown, closely followed by Lafayette and von Steuben.

Here was a great opportunity, and Washington seized it. Joined by Rochambeau from Rhode Island and informed that a large French fleet under the Comte de Grasse was sailing for Virginia, Washington secretly began to move the bulk of his army south. Making a feint towards New York to deceive Clinton, he moved into Virginia. De Grasse arrived at the end of August, blockaded Chesapeake Bay, and landed his troops to join Lafayette. A British fleet under Admiral Thomas Graves tried to break the blockade on September 5 but was defeated and withdrew to New York, abandoning Cornwallis. Washington arrived and with his allied army of about 16,000 laid siege to the town. Without access to the sea the British were doomed, and Cornwallis knew it. On October 19, with his band playing "The World Turned Upside Down," he surrendered his entire army, and wrote to Clinton: "I have the mortification to inform your Excellency that I have been forced to give up the posts of York and Gloucester, and to surrender the troops under my command, by capitulation on the 19th inst. as prisoners of war to the combined forces of America and France."

Ironically, on October 24 Clinton arrived off the coast with 7,000 reinforcements, but on learning of the British surrender sailed back to New York. Washington now urged a joint attack on New York but de Grasse, pleading he was already overdue in the West Indies, refused to participate. Washington then marched northward to keep up the envelopment of New York while Rochambeau spent the winter in Virginia, returned to his base in Rhode Island the following fall, and sailed for France in December.

Cornwallis' surrender, combined with French victories in the West Indies in late 1781 and early 1782, convinced the British that they must sue for peace. In March Parliament passed an act authorizing the Crown to start peace negotiations with the former colonies. In April preliminary talks began in Paris with Benjamin Franklin, later joined by John

Revolutionary powder horn and canteen.

Uniforms of French soldiers in America.

Adams, John Jay, and Henry Laurens. Formal negotiations commenced in September, and in November the American representatives signed the preliminary Articles of Peace, ratified by Congress the following April, although the official signing of the treaty did not take place until September 1783 in Paris. Due to the tenacity and stubbornness of the American peace envoys, the United States achieved its principal objectives: independence, adequate boundaries, free access to international waterways, the right to fish off Newfoundland and Nova Scotia, and the evacuation of British land and sea forces. The last British troops, now commanded by Sir Guy Carleton, sailed from New York that December.

"It will not be believed," Washington wrote, "that such a force as Great Britain has employed for eight years in this country could be baffled in the plan of subjugating it, by numbers infinitely less, composed of men oftentimes

Surrender of Cornwallis at Yorktown, by John Trumbull.

Mustered out—a rest on the way home. Painting by Howard Pyle.
(*"Harper's Magazine,"* Sept. 1896)

half starved, always in rags, without pay, and experiencing every species of distress which human nature is capable of undergoing."

Sad to relate, their distress did not cease with their discharge. Congress gratefully voted each soldier a bonus of $80, but then had to issue certificates or I.O.U.'s in lieu of money because of its destitute financial condition. Many of the soldiers sold their certificates for a pittance to speculators to help feed or clothe themselves on the way home. Most of them, however, left "without the settlement of their accounts or a farthing of money in their pockets." They straggled home in groups, ragged and dirty, hungry, tired, and sick, begging meals at taverns and farmhouses or stealing a chicken here and there.

It was a bitter homecoming, and yet these veterans generally were not bitter. They were rugged individuals as well as individualists, and from their diaries and letters it appears they were genuine patriots, well aware of what they had been fighting and dying for, with the astounding patience and fortitude to suffer through unbelievable hardship until British blunders and French assistance gave them victory in the end. They had won, and in so doing had accomplished the seemingly impossible. Whether they realized it or not, they were the instrument by which the great principle that men make governments was realized; the instrument by which the traditional belief in the divine right of kings was finally repudiated. Their commander in chief summed up for them the real meaning of what they had accomplished:

The Citizens of America, placed in the most enviable condition, as the sole Lords and Proprietors of a vast tract of Continent, comprehending all the various soils and climates of the World, and abounding with all the necessaries and conveniences of life, are now by the late satisfactory pacification, acknowledged to be possessed of absolute freedom and Independency; They are, from this period, to be considered as the Actors on a most conspicuous Theatre, which seems to be peculiarly designated by Providence for the display of human greatness and felicity; Here, they are not only surrounded with every thing which can contribute to the completion of private and domestic enjoyment, but Heaven has crowned all its other blessings, by giving a fairer opportunity for political happiness, than any other Nation has ever been favored with . . . for with our fate will the destiny of unborn Millions be involved.

The world had, indeed, been turned upside down.

Suggested Readings

Commager, Henry S. & Morris, Richard, eds. *The Spirit of 'Seventy-Six,* 2 volumes, New York, 1958.

Scheer, George F. & Rankin, Hugh F. *Rebels and Redcoats,* New York, 1957.

Ward, Christopher. *The War of the Revolution,* 2 volumes, New York, 1952.

Wallace, Willard M. *Appeal to Arms,* New York, 1951.

Montross, Lynn. *The Reluctant Rebels,* New York, 1950.

Miller, John C. *Origins of the American Revolution,* Boston, 1943.

Scott, John A., ed. *The Diary of the American Revolution,* New York, 1967.

Van Doren, Carl. *Secret History of the American Revolution,* New York, 1941.

Morris, Richard. *The American Revolution Reconsidered,* New York, 1967.

Callahan, North. *Flight From The Republic,* New York, 1967.

Galvin, John R. *The Minute Men,* New York, 1967.

Index

(Note: Page numbers in italics refer to illustrations and/or their captions.)

ADAMS, John, 26, 30, 57, *70*, 119
Adams, Samuel, 8, *9*, 12, 19, 20, 21, 26, 27, 28, 30
Albany (N.Y.), 84, 86, 87
Alexander, Brig. Gen. William (Lord Stirling), *67*
Allen, Maj. Gen. (Vt. militia) Ethan, 29
Alliance (USS), 99
Amboy (N.J.), 83
Appalachian Mountains, 59, 101
Arnold, Maj. Gen. Benedict, 28, 29, 39, 41, 53, *73*, 85, *86;* in Virginia, 116
Arthurs, Stanley M. (artist), *37*
Articles of Peace, 119
Attucks, Crispus, *62*
Augusta (Ga.), 103

BACON'S Rebellion (1676), 17
Baltic Sea, 96
Barry, Capt. John (USN), *99*
Bemis Heights (Stillwater, N.Y.), 87
Bennington (Vt.), Battle of, *85*
Bonhomme Richard (USS), *98*, 99
Bordentown (N.J.), 76
Boston (Mass.), 7, 8, 14, 15, 19, 22, 27, 28, 29, 30, 31, 32, 36, 45, *48*, *50*, 60, 65, 92, 96, 97
Boston Massacre, 12, *20*
Boston Port Act, 22
Boston Tea Party, 12, 22, *23*
Brandywine Creek (Pa.), Battle of, *88-89*
Breach, the, 52
Breed's Hill, 32, *33*
British Legion (cavalry), *110*
Brooklyn Heights, 65, 67, 70
Brooklyn (N.Y.), 65, 66
Brumidi, Constantino (artist), *20*
Bunker Hill, *31*, 32; casualties, 34; 36, 49, 62, 67
Burgoyne, Maj. Gen. John, *32;* to invade from Canada, 83, 84; *83*, *84*, 85, 86; surrenders to Gates, *87*

CAHOKIA, 101
Cambridge (Mass.), 15, 28, 31, 35
Camden (S.C.), Battle of, *109*, 113
Cape Fear (N.C.), 45, 48
Carleton, Maj. Gen. Sir Guy, 36, *37*, 38, 39, 40, 54, 72, 74, 119
Channing, Edward, 52
Chapman, Carlton T. (artist), *72-73*
Chappel, Alonzo (artist), *10*, *78*, *85*, *91*, *107,115*
Charleston (S.C.), 22, 45, 48, 51, 55, 62, 103, 105, *107*, 116
Charlestown (Mass.), 32
Chaudiere River, 39
Chesapeake Bay, 88, 117
Clark, Col. George Rogers, 101, *102*, 103
Clark, Rev. Jonas, 12
Clinton, Maj. Gen. Henry, 31, 32, 45, *47*, 51, 52, 55, 85, 87, 95, 96, 103, 104, 107, 108, 115, 117, 118
Coercive (Intolerable) Acts, 22
Committees of Correspondence, 20
Common Sense, (pamphlet by Thomas Paine), 42
Concord (Mass.), 7, 8, 9, *11*, 12, 13, 28
Concord River, 13
Continental Army, 31, 62, 63, *71;* condition during 1776-77 winter, 76; *79;* number, pay, and uniforms, 80; rations, medicines, and diseases, 81, 82; recreations, 82; at Valley Forge, 90 *ff.;* morale, 92*ff.;* 103, 108, 109; mutiny, 112; 114
Continental Association, 26
Continental Navy, 97
Copley, John Singleton (artist), *9*
Corbin, Molly, 64
Cornwallis, Maj. Gen. Lord Charles, 45, 51, 55, 75, 76, 77, 78, 108; at Camden (S.C.), 109; 110, 113, *114*, 115, 116, 117; surrender at Yorktown (Va.), 118, *120-121*
Cowpens (S.C.), Battle of, 114, *115*
Cromwell, Oliver, 63

125

Crown Point (N.Y.), 37

DAN River, 114
Darley, Felix O. C. (artist), *7*
Dawes, William, 8
Dead River, 39
Declaration of Independence, *56*, *57*, 58, 60, *61*, 70
Declaration of Rights, 26
Delaware River, 63, *75*, 76, 77, 88
Des Barres, Joseph F. W. (artist), *55*
Diseases of soldiers, 82
Ditzlar, H. (artist), *94*
Dorchester Heights (Boston), 32, *48*, 65
Dunsmore, John Ward (artist), *70*

EARL, Ralph (artist),*93*
East India Company, 21
East River (N.Y.), 65, 66, 67, 68, 71
Estaing, Adm. Charles Hector Théodat, comte d', 96, *103*, 104

FERGUSON, Maj. Patrick, 110
First Continental Congress, 23, 26
First North Carolina Regiment, 47
Fly (USS), 98
Fort Johnson, 51
Fort Lee, 71, 75
Fort Moultrie (Sullivan), *51*, 52
Fort Sackville, 102
Fort Stanwix, 85
Fort Sullivan (Moultrie), *51*, 52
Fort Ticonderoga, *28*, 37, 39, 48, 54, 75, 84
Fort Washington, 64, 71; capture of, 75
Franklin, Benjamin, 44, *70*, 118
French Alliance, 88, 95, 99, 102

GAGE, Maj. Gen. Thomas, 27, 31, 32; re-called, 36
Gates, Maj. Gen. Horatio, *86*; receives Burgoyne's surrender, *87*; given com-mand in South, 109; relieved, 110
George III, King, 19, 22, 23, *25*, 26, 30, 42, 46
Georgia militia, 62
Germantown (Pa.), Battle of, *90*
Gibault, Father Pierre, 102
Glover, Brig. Gen. John, *68*
Grasse, Adm. François Joseph Paul, comte de, 117, 118
Graves, Adm. Thomas, 117
Gravesend (Long Island, N.Y.), 66
Greene, Maj. Gen. Nathanael, 71, 75, 109; given command in South, 110; *113*, 114
Green Mountain Boys, *29*
Griffin, Edward, 63
Groton (Mass.), 64
Guan, Heights of, 65
Guilford Court House (N.C.), Battle of, 114, *116*

HACKENSACK (N.J.), 75, 76
Halifax (N.S.), 50, 54
Hamilton, Gov. Henry, 102, 103
Hancock, John, 8, *9*, 12, 28
Hannah (privateer), 97
Hanover, royal house of, 46
Harlem Heights (N.Y.), 70, *71*
Hays, Mary, 64
Head of Elk (Md.), 8
Heights of Guan, 65
Henry, Gov. Patrick, 20, 101
Hessians, 55, 64, 72, 76; at Trenton, 77; *84*
Highland Scots, 46, 47
Hopkins, C. in C. of Continental Navy Esek, 98
Hornet (USS), 98
Howe, Adm. Richard, 55, *66*; at Newport (R.I.), 96
Howe, Maj. Gen. Sir William, 31, 32, 34; takes command, 36; *38*, 46, 49, 50, 51, 54, 55, 56; at Battle of Long Island, 66; 67, 69, *70*, 71, 74, 76, 77, 83, 84, 85, 88, 89, 95, 108
Hudson River, 37, *74*, 75, 84, 86, 87
Huguenots, 60

INDIANS, 36, 60, 62, 72, 79, *84*, 101
Intolerable (Coercive) Acts, 22, 26
Irish-Americans, 60
Iroquois Indians, 62

JAMES Island (Charleston, S.C.), 51, 107
Jamestown (Va.), 17
Jay, John, 119
Jefferson, Thomas, 20, *21*, 42; drafts Decla-ration of Independence, *58*
Jews in Revolution, 62
Jones, Capt. John Paul (USN), *95*, 98, 99

KASKASKIA, 101, 102
Kennebec River (Maine), 39
King's Mountain (Carolinas border), Battle of, 110, *111*, 114, 115
Kip's Bay (N.Y.), 70
Knox, Maj. Gen. Henry, 48, *49*

LAFAYETTE, Maj. Gen. Marie Joseph Paul Yves Roch Gilbert du Motier, marquis de, in Virginia, *117*
Lake Champlain, 28, 38, 73, 83
Lake George, 38
Lake Megantic, 39
Lancaster (Pa.) 89
Laurens, Henry, 119
Lee, Maj. Gen. Charles, 30, 95
Lee, Richard Henry, 20; introduces inde-pendence resolution, 57
Letters of marque, 96
Leutz, Emanuel (artist), *75*
Lexington (Mass.), 7, 8, *10*, 12

Lincoln, Maj. Gen. Benjamin, 103, 107
"Lobsterback," 20
Long Island (Isle of Palms, Charleston, S.C.), 52
Long Island (N.Y.), 65; Battle of, 66, 89
Long Island Sound (N.Y.), 71
Lovell, Tom (artist), *49*
Loyalists (Tories), 45, 46, 47, 50, 52, 58, *59*, 64, 84, 92, 95, 101, 103, 110, 114, 115

McBARRON, H. Charles, Jr. (artist), *50*
McDonald, Donald, 46
Machias (Maine), 97
Manhattan Island (N.Y.), 65, 70
Marblehead (Mass.), 68
Marines, 97
Martin, Royal Gov. Josiah (N.C.), 45, 46
Massachusetts Assembly, 19
Medicines for soldiers, 81
Militia, difficulties with, 79
Minutemen, at Concord, 13, 14, 15; in North Carolina, 47
"Minutewomen," 64
Mississippi River, 101
Mohawk Valley (N.Y.), 84, 85
"Molly Pitcher," *64*
Money, *59*, 92
Monmouth (N.J.), 63, *64*; Battle of, *94*, 95
Montgomery, Brig. Gen. Richard, *38*, 39, *41*
Montreal (Canada), 38, 39, 54
Moore, Col. James, 47
Moore's Creek (N.C.), *46*, 47, 52
Morgan, Brig. Gen. Daniel, *37*; in South, 113, 114
Morristown (N.J.), 78, *106*, 112
Morse, Samuel F. B. (artist), *9*
Moultrie, Maj. Gen. William, 51

NASSAU (Bahamas), 98
Negroes in Revolution, 62, 63
New Brunswick (N.J.), 76, 78
Newfoundland, 119
Newport (R.I.), 64, 96, 108, 109
New York (N.Y.), 22, 50, 51, 52, 54, *55*, 56, 60, 65, 67, 68, 76, 83, 85, 87, 88, 95, 96, 103, 105, 108, 117, 118, 119
Niagara, 101
Nicholson, Capt. James (USN), 99
North Bridge (*Concord*, Mass.), *13*
North Castle (N.Y.), 71
North, Lord Frederick, 21
North River (N.Y.), 50
Northwest, the, 101, 102, 103
Nova Scotia, 119

OGDEN, Henry A. (artist), *36*, *87*
Ohio River, 101
"Olive Branch Petition," 42
Oswego (N.Y.), 84

Otis, Bass (artist), *43*
Ozanne, Pierre (artist), *97*

PAINE, Thomas, 42, *43*, 76, 77
Palisades (Hudson River), 71, 75
Paris (France), 119
Parker, Adm. Peter, *45*, 51, 52, 55
Parker, Capt. John, 9, 11, 12
Parliament, 18, 20, 22, 23, 26, 43, 118
Patriots, 46, 47, 110, 114
Peale, Charles Willson (artist), *74*, *95*
Peixotto, E. C. (artist), *98*
Pell's Point (N.Y.), 71
Pennsylvania Executive Council, 112
Pennsylvania Germans, 60
Philadelphia (Pa.), 22, 23, 28, 30, 42, 43, 47, 84, 85, 88, 89, 90, *91*, 93, 95, 112
Phillips, Maj. Gen. William, 116
Piedmont district (N.C.), 46
Pitcairn, Maj. John, 8, 9, 10, 11, 62
Plan, British, for subduing colonies, 44
Prescott, Col. William, 32
Prescott, Dr. Samuel, 8
Princeton (N.J.), 76; Battle of, *78*
Punkatasset Hill (Concord, Mass.), 13
Putnam, Maj. Gen. Israel, 32, *65*, 66
Pyle, Howard (artist), *21*, *27*, *33*, *59*, *61*, *62*, *71*, *122*

QUAKERS, 60
Quebec (Canada), expedition route, 39, *53*, 54

RALEIGH Tavern (Williamsburg, Va.), 19
Ranger (USS), 99
Rattlesnake (privateer), 96
Redstone Fort, 101
Reid, Robert (artist), *23*
Revere, Paul, *8*
Richmond (Va.), 116
Rifles, *82*
Robertson, Archibald (artist), *54*
Rochambeau, Lt. Gen. Jean Baptiste Donatien de Vimeur, comte de, *108*, 117, 118
Rush, Dr. Benjamin, 82
Rutledge, Edmund, *70*

St. Johns (Canada), 38, 39
St. Lawrence River, 37, 39
Salem, Peter, 62, *63*
Salomon, Haym, 62
Salvador, Francis, 62
Saratoga (N.Y.), *86*, 87, 90, 109
Savannah (Ga.), 103, *104-105*
Schuyler, Maj. Gen. Philip, 37, 39, 84
Schuylkill River, 89, 90
Scotch-Irish, 46, 110
Second Continental Congress, 28, 30, 31, 35, 36, 40, 42, 47, 53, 56; acts on Declaration of Independence, 58; 62, 63, 69,

The Call of the Wild

Jack London

Illustrations by Philippe Munch

Viking

CONTENTS

1   Into the Primitive   7

2   The Law of Club and Fang   25

3   The Dominant Primordial Beast   39

4   Who Has Won to Mastership   57

5   The Toil of Trace and Trail   67

6   For the Love of a Man   85

7   The Sounding of the Call   101

1

INTO THE PRIMITIVE

Old longings nomadic leap
Chafing at custom's chain;
Again from its brumal sleep
Wakens the ferine strain.

Buck did not read the newspapers, or he would have known that trouble was brewing not alone for himself, but for every tide-water dog, strong of muscle and with warm, long hair, from Puget Sound to San Diego. Because men, groping in the arctic darkness, had found a yellow metal, and because steamship and transportation companies were booming the find, thousands of men were rushing into the Northland. These men wanted dogs, and the dogs they wanted were heavy dogs, with strong muscles by which to toil and furry coats to protect them from the frost.

Buck lived at a big house in the sun-kissed Santa Clara Valley. Judge Miller's place, it was called. It stood back from the road, half-hidden among the trees, through which glimpses could be caught of the

7

The Klondike News (*above*) features gold hunter George Washington Carmack on its front page. In August 1896, in tiny Rabbit Creek, Carmack had found a vein "thick as a hunk of cheese between two slices of bread." His first day's haul was 20 ounces (600 grams); the amount rose with each succeeding day. The press quickly spread news of his sudden wealth worldwide. Taking advantage of this gold fever, an ad (*below*) uses the miners' reputation for heavy smoking to extol the flavor of Smith & Sons Tobacco.

wide cool veranda that ran around its four sides. The house was approached by graveled driveways which wound about through wide-spreading lawns and under the interlacing boughs of tall poplars. At the rear things were on even a more spacious scale than at the front. There were great stables, where a dozen grooms and boys held forth, rows of vine-clad servants' cottages, an endless and orderly array of outhouses, long grape arbors, green pastures, orchards, and berry patches. Then there was the pumping plant for the artesian well, and the big cement tank where Judge Miller's boys took their morning plunge and kept cool in the hot afternoon.

And over this great demesne Buck ruled. Here he was born and here he had lived the four years of his life. It was true, there were other dogs. There could not but be other dogs on so vast a place, but they did not count. They came and went, resided in the populous kennels, or lived obscurely in the recesses of the house after the fashion of Toots, the Japanese pug,

❝ And over this great demesne Buck ruled. Here he was born and here he had lived the four years of his life. The whole realm was his. ❞

or Ysabel, the Mexican hairless—strange creatures that rarely put nose out of doors or set foot to ground. On the other hand, there were the fox terriers, a score of them at least, who yelped fearful promises at Toots and Ysabel looking out of the windows at them and protected by a legion of housemaids armed with brooms and mops.

But Buck was neither house-dog nor kennel-dog. The whole realm was his. He plunged into the swimming tank or went hunting with the Judge's sons; he escorted Mollie and Alice, the Judge's daughters, on long twilight or early morning rambles; on wintry nights he lay at the Judge's feet before the roaring library fire; he carried the Judge's grandsons on his back, or rolled them in the grass, and guarded their footsteps through wild adventures down to the fountain in the stable yard, and even beyond, where the paddocks were, and the berry patches. Among the terriers he stalked imperiously, and Toots and Ysabel he utterly ignored, for he was king—king over all the creeping,

The collie, which is sturdy and can tolerate harsh climates, is ideally suited to act as a sled dog in the mountains. However, it was replaced by the husky, the dog originally used by the Arctic natives.

9

The Bulletin's front page announces "The Best Road to the Klondike"—the White Pass, so called because the first photos showed it under a blanket of snow.

crawling, flying things of Judge Miller's place, humans included.

His father, Elmo, a huge St. Bernard, had been the Judge's inseparable companion and Buck did fair to follow in the way of his father. He was not so large—he weighed only one hundred and forty pounds—for his mother, Shep, had been a Scotch shepherd dog. Nevertheless, one hundred and forty pounds, to which was added the dignity that comes of good living and universal respect, enabled him to carry himself in right royal fashion. During the four years since his puppyhood he had lived the life of a sated aristocrat; he had a fine pride in himself, was ever a trifle egotistical, as country gentlemen sometimes become because of their insular situation. But he had saved himself by not becoming a mere pampered house-dog. Hunting and kindred outdoor delights had kept down the fat and hardened his muscles; and to him, as to the cold-tubbing races, the love of water had been a tonic and a health preserver.

And this was the manner of dog Buck was in the fall of 1897, when the Klondike strike dragged men from all the world into the frozen North. But Buck did not read the newspapers, and he did not know that Manuel, one of the gardener's helpers, was an undesirable acquaintance. Manuel had one besetting sin. He loved to play Chinese lottery. Also, in his gambling, he had one besetting weakness—faith in a system;

and this made his damnation certain. For to play a system requires money, while the wages of a gardener's helper do not lap over the needs of a wife and numerous progeny.

The Judge was at a meeting of the Raisin Growers' Association, and the boys were busy organizing an athletic club, on the memorable night of Manuel's treachery. No one saw him and Buck go off through the orchard on what Buck imagined was merely a stroll. And with the exception of a solitary man, no one saw them arrive at the little flag station known as College Park. This man talked with Manuel, and money clinked between them.

"You might wrap up the goods before you deliver 'm," the stranger said gruffly, and Manuel doubled a piece of stout rope around Buck's neck under the collar.

"Twist it, an' you'll choke 'm plentee," said Manuel, and the stranger grunted a ready affirmative.

Buck had accepted the rope with quiet dignity. To be sure, it was an unwonted performance: but he had learned to trust in men he knew, and to give them credit for a wisdom that outreached his own. But when the ends of the rope were placed in the stranger's hands, he growled menacingly. He had merely intimated his displeasure, in his pride believing that to intimate was to

❝ Manuel had one besetting sin. He loved to play Chinese lottery. ❞

For the construction of the transcontinental railway (1861–1869) America looked to China for cheap labor. Chinese men who arrived in California later sent for their families, and throve in business—laundries, restaurants, and other trade, not all of it legal. Many Chinese settled in the section of San Francisco shown above, which they inhabit to this day. The picture below shows a secret Chinese gambling den.

❝ This man talked with Manuel, and money clinked between them. ❞

11

THE KLONDIKE

Jack London in the Klondike

At age 14, Jack London first encountered the working world, in a San Francisco cannery; a life of drifting and adventure opened up to him. He joined militant socialists in denouncing worker exploitation and unemployment in California. At the first rumors of Klondike gold, London left San Francisco, on July 25, 1897. He arrived at Dyea on August 7 and left the Chilkoot Pass on August 30, with the first snowfall. He and four companions built a small boat which they launched on the Yukon. Reaching Upper Island, the five men started prospecting, confident they would soon find gold. London, however, gave up and returned to Dawson City, where he barely survived an attack of the disease scurvy. He left with the thaw, on June 8. Though he hadn't grown rich, London had discovered the wilderness. He would draw on the dozens of stories he picked up, true and false, as material for many of his novels: *The Call of the Wild* (1903), followed by *The Sea–Wolf, White Fang* and *Daughter of the Snows.*

13

For Americans, Klondike gold offered a rare chance to "get rich quick." The memory of successful miners in California in 1849 and 1850 was still very much alive. Trains quickly filled up with all the castoffs of industrial society. The fever even reached Europe.

command. But to his surprise the rope tightened around his neck, shutting off his breath. In quick rage he sprang at the man, who met him halfway, grappled him close by the throat, and with a deft twist threw him over on his back. Then the rope tightened mercilessly, while Buck struggled in a fury, his tongue lolling out of his mouth and his great chest panting futilely. Never in all his life had he been so vilely treated, and never in all his life had he been so angry. But his strength ebbed, his eyes glazed, and he knew nothing when the train was flagged and the two men threw him into the baggage car.

The next he knew, he was dimly aware that his tongue was hurting and that he was being jolted along in some kind of conveyance. The hoarse shriek of a locomotive whistling a crossing told him where he was. He had traveled too often with the Judge not to know the sensation of riding in a baggage car. He opened his eyes, and into them came the unbridled anger of a kidnapped king. The man sprang for his throat, but Buck was too quick for him. His jaws closed on the hand; nor did they relax till his senses were choked out of him once more.

"Yep, has fits," the man said, hiding his mangled hand from the baggageman, who had been attracted by the sounds of struggle. "I'm takin' 'im up for the boss to 'Frisco. A crack dog-doctor there thinks that he can cure 'im."

Concerning that night's ride the man spoke most eloquently for himself, in a little shed back of a saloon on the San Francisco water front.

❝ The next he knew, he was dimly aware that his tongue was hurting and that he was being jolted along in some kind of conveyance. ❞

"All I get is fifty for it," he grumbled; "an' I wouldn't do it over for a thousand, cold cash."

His hand was wrapped in a bloody handkerchief, and the right trouser leg was ripped from knee to ankle.

"How much did the other mug get?" the saloon-keeper demanded.

"A hundred," was the reply. "Wouldn't take a sou less, so help me."

"That makes a hundred and fifty," the saloon-keeper calculated, "and he's worth it, or I'm a square-head."

The kidnapper undid the bloody wrappings and looked at his lacerated hand. "If I don't get the hydrophoby—"

"It'll be because you were born to hang," laughed the saloon-keeper. "Here, lend me a hand before you pull your freight," he added.

Dazed, suffering intolerable pain from throat and tongue, with the life half throttled out of him, Buck attempted to face his tormentors. But he was thrown down and choked repeatedly, till they succeeded in filing the heavy brass collar from off his neck. Then the rope was removed, and he was flung into a cage-like crate.

There he lay for the remainder of the weary night, nursing his wrath and wounded pride. He could not understand what it all meant. What did they want with him, these strange men? Why were they keeping him pent up in this narrow crate? He did not know why, but he felt oppressed by the vague sense of impending calamity. Several times during the night he sprang to his feet when the shed door rattled open, expecting to see the Judge, or the boys at least. But each time it was the bulging face of the saloon-keeper that peered in at him by the sickly light of a tallow candle. And each time the joyful bark that trembled in Buck's throat was twisted into a savage growl.

But the saloon-keeper let him alone, and in the morning four men entered and picked up the crate. More tormentors,

❝ In quick rage he sprang at the man, who met him halfway, grappled him close by the throat, and with a deft twist threw him over on his back. **❞**

In San Francisco, some cafés served as more-or-less secret stock exchanges. The cellar of the café shown above has posted daily rates for gold and silver from the mines of the American West. The room is packed— some people are gambling, and all are dreaming of making fortunes.

Buck decided, for they were evil-looking creatures, ragged and unkempt; and he stormed and raged at them through the bars. They only laughed and poked sticks at him, which he promptly assailed with his teeth till he

realized that that was what they wanted. Whereupon he lay down sullenly and allowed the crate to be lifted into a wagon. Then he, and the crate in which he was imprisoned, began a passage through many hands. Clerks in the express office took charge of him; he was carted about in another wagon; a truck carried him, with an assortment of boxes and parcels, upon a ferry steamer; he was trucked off the steamer into a great railway depot, and finally he was deposited in an express car.

No one wanted to miss out on the chance to hit the gold jackpot. However uncomfortable the journey—the long days crossing the American continent to reach the forests of the Northwest, the bad food, thieving,

For two days and nights this express car was dragged along at the tail of shrieking locomotives; and for two days and nights Buck neither ate nor drank. In his anger he had met the first advances of the express messengers with growls, and they had retaliated by teasing him. When he flung himself against the

bars, quivering and frothing, they laughed at him and taunted him. They growled and barked like detestable dogs, mewed, and flapped their arms and crowed. It was all very silly, he knew; but therefore the more outrage to his dignity, and his anger waxed and waxed. He did not mind the hunger so much, but the lack of water caused him severe suffering and fanned his wrath to fever-pitch. For that matter, high-strung and

and brawls—people piled into the berths of the trains, dreaming of gold nuggets. Hordes came, and the best places were quickly snatched up.

finely sensitive, the ill treatment had flung him into a fever, which was fed by the inflammation of his parched and swollen throat and tongue.

He was glad for one thing: the rope was off his neck. That had given them an unfair advantage; but now that it was

off, he would show them. They would never get another rope around his neck. Upon that he was resolved. For two days and nights he neither ate nor drank and during those two days and nights of torment, he accumulated a fund of wrath that boded ill for whoever first fell foul of him. His eyes turned bloodshot, and he was metamorphosed into a raging fiend. So changed was he that the Judge himself would not have recognized him; and the express messengers breathed with relief when they bundled him off the train at Seattle.

Four men gingerly carried the crate from the wagon into a small, high-walled backyard. A stout man, with a red sweater that sagged generously at the neck, came out and signed the book for the driver. That was the man, Buck divined, the next tormentor, and he hurled himself savagely against the bars. The man smiled grimly, and brought a hatchet and a club.

THE SEATTLE POST-INTELLIGENCER.

LATEST NEWS FROM THE KLONDIKE.
9 O'CLOCK EDITION.

"Gold! Gold! Gold! Gold!": A Seattle newspaper gives the latest news from the Klondike. The great port city is well situated near Tacoma, the last stop of the Northern Pacific transcontinental railway line. Since the United States purchased Alaska from Russia in 1867, Seattle has been a hub of American commerce.

66 A stout man, with a red sweater that sagged generously at the neck, came out and signed the book for the driver. That was the man, Buck divined, the next tormentor. 99

"You ain't going to take him out now?" the driver asked.

"Sure," the man replied, driving the hatchet into the crate for a pry.

There was an instantaneous scattering of the four men who had carried it in, and from safe perches on top the wall they prepared to watch the performance.

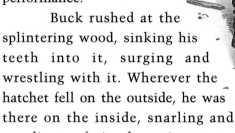

Buck rushed at the splintering wood, sinking his teeth into it, surging and wrestling with it. Wherever the hatchet fell on the outside, he was there on the inside, snarling and growling, as furiously anxious to get out as the man in the red sweater was calmly intent on getting him out.

"Now, you red-eyed devil," he said, when he had made an opening sufficient for the passage of Buck's body. At the same time he dropped the hatchet and shifted the club to his right hand.

And Buck was truly a red-eyed devil, as he drew himself together for the spring, hair bristling, mouth foaming, a mad glitter in his bloodshot eyes. Straight at the man he launched his one hundred and forty pounds of fury, surcharged with the pent passion of two days and nights. In midair, just as his jaws were about to close on the man, he received a shock that checked his body and brought his teeth together with an agonizing clip. He whirled over, fetching the ground on his back and side. He had never been struck by a club in his life, and did not understand. With a snarl that was part bark and more scream he was again on his feet and launched into the air. And again the shock came and

From the moment gold was discovered in Alaska's Yukon Valley in 1890, "ground scrapers," as the miners were called, scoured the region, giving rise to trade relations between the Yukon and the Washington State ports of Tacoma and Seattle, which were loading sites for materials and supplies such as grain that could not be grown in the far north. *Above,* a street in Tacoma.

❝ 'Now, you red-eyed devil,' he said, when he had made an opening sufficient for the passage of Buck's body. At the same time he dropped the hatchet and shifted the club to his right hand.❞

he was brought crushingly to the ground. This time he was aware that it was the club, but his madness knew no caution. A dozen times he charged, and as often the club broke the charge and smashed him down.

After a particularly fierce blow, he crawled to his feet, too dazed to rush. He staggered limply about, the blood flowing from nose and mouth and ears, his beautiful coat sprayed and flecked with bloody slaver. Then the man advanced and deliberately dealt him a frightful blow on the nose. All the pain he had endured was as nothing compared with the exquisite agony of this. With a roar that was almost lionlike in its ferocity, he again hurled himself at the man. But the man, shifting the club from right to left, cooly caught him by the underjaw, at the same time wrenching downward and backward. Buck described a complete circle in the air, and half of another, then crashed to the ground on his head and chest.

For the last time he rushed. The man struck the shrewd blow he had purposely withheld for so long, and Buck crumpled up and went down, knocked utterly senseless.

"He's no slouch at dog-breakin', that's wot I say," one of the men on the wall cried enthusiastically.

A street in Tacoma lined with crates and sacks of flour ready to be loaded onto boats bound for the Klondike. In the background we see Cooper & Levy's store, which offered pioneers and miners sturdy, practical clothing.

66 A dozen times he charged, and as often the club broke the charge and smashed him down. 99

"Druther break cayuses any day, and twice on Sundays," was the reply of the driver, as he climbed on the wagon and started the horses.

Buck's senses came back to him, but not his strength. He lay where he had fallen, and from there he watched the man in the red sweater.

"'Answers to the name of Buck,'" the man soliloquized, quoting from the saloon-keeper's letter which had announced the consignment of the crate and contents. "Well, Buck, my boy," he went on in a genial voice, "we've had our little ruction, and the best thing we can do is to let it go at that. You've learned your place, and I know mine. Be a good dog and all 'll go well and the goose hang high. Be a bad dog, and I'll whale the stuffin' outa you. Understand?"

As he spoke he fearlessly patted the head he had so mercilessly pounded, and though Buck's hair involuntarily bristled at touch of the hand, he endured it without protest. When the man brought him water he drank eagerly, and later bolted a generous meal of raw meat, chunk by chunk, from the man's hand.

He was beaten (he knew that); but he was not broken. He saw, once for all, that he stood no chance against a man with a club. He had learned the lesson, and in all his after life he never forgot it. That club was a revelation. It was his introduction to the reign of primitive law, and he met the introduction halfway. The facts of life took on a fiercer aspect; and while he faced that aspect uncowed, he faced it with all the

DATE OF ISSUE *Mar 30/98*   No. 14271

DOMINION of CANADA

FREE MINER'S CERTIFICATE.

PLACE OF ISSUE VANCOUVER B.C. NON-TRANSFERABLE.   VALID FOR ONE YEAR ONLY.

This is to Certify that E. James de Lequart of James Francis has paid me this day the sum of Five Dollars and is entitled to all the rights and privileges of a Free Miner, under any Mining Regulations of the Government of Canada, for one year from the 30 day of March 18...

This Certificate shall also grant to the holder thereof the privilege of Fishing and Shooting, subject to the provisions of any Act which has been passed, or which may hereafter be passed for the protection of game and fish; also the privilege of Cutting Timber for actual necessities, for building houses, boats, and for general mining operations; such timber, however, to be for the exclusive use of the miner himself, but such permission shall not extend to timber which may have been heretofore or which may hereafter be granted to other persons or corporations.

Countersigned

Certificat de Mineur Libre, délivré par le Gouvernement canadien.

Since the Klondike's land and subsoil belong to the state of Canada, every miner had to be registered, which required paying a small licensing fee. In exchange, the government guaranteed him the rights to hunt, fish, build, and mine within the limits of the law.

❝ 'Well, Buck, my boy,' he went on in a genial voice, 'we've had our little ruction, and the best thing we can do is to let it go at that. You've learned your place, and I know mine.' ❞

latent cunning of his nature aroused. As the days went by, other dogs came, in crates and at the ends of ropes, some docilely, and some raging and roaring as he had come; and, one and all, he watched them pass under the dominion of the man in the red sweater. Again and again, as he looked at each brutal performance, the lesson was driven home to Buck: a man with a club was a law-giver, a master to be obeyed, though not necessarily con-ciliated. Of this last Buck was never guilty, though he did see beaten dogs that fawned upon the man, and wagged their tails, and licked his hand. Also he saw one dog, that would neither conciliate nor obey, finally killed in the struggle for mastery.

Now and again men came, strangers, who talked excitedly, wheedlingly, and in all kinds of fashions to the man in the red sweater. And at such times that money passed between them the strangers took one or more of the dogs away with them. Buck wondered where they went, for they never came back; but the fear of the future was strong upon him, and he was glad each time when he was not selected.

Yet his time came, in the end, in the form of a little weazened man who spat broken English and many strange and

> **"** Now and again men came, strangers, who talked excitedly to the man in the red sweater. **"**

21

uncouth exclamations which Buck could not understand.

"Sacredam!" he cried, when his eyes lit upon Buck. "Dat one dam bully dog! Eh? How moch?"

"Three hundred, and a present at that," was the prompt reply of the man in the red sweater. "And seein' it's government money, you ain't got no kick coming; eh, Perrault?"

Perrault grinned. Considering that the price of dogs had been boomed skyward by the unwonted demand, it was not an unfair sum for so fine an animal. The Canadian Government would be no loser, nor would its dispatches travel the slower. Perrault knew dogs, and when he looked at Buck he knew that he was one in a thousand—"One in ten t'ousand," he commented mentally.

Buck saw money pass between them, and was not surprised when Curly, a good-natured Newfoundland, and he were led away by the little weazened man. That was the last he saw of the man in the red sweater, and as Curly and he looked at receding Seattle from the deck of the *Narwhal*, it was the last he saw of the warm Southland. Curly and he were taken below by Perrault and turned over to a black-faced giant called François. Perrault was a French-Canadian, and swarthy; but François was a French-Canadian half-breed, and twice as swarthy. They were a new kind of men to Buck (of which he was destined to see many more), and while he developed no affection for them, he none the less grew honestly to respect them. He speedily learned that Perrault and François were fair men, calm and impartial in administering justice, and too wise in the way of dogs to be ever fooled by dogs.

In the 'tween-decks of the *Narwhal*, Buck and Curly joined two other dogs. One of them was a big, snow-white fellow from Spitzbergen who had been brought away by a whaling captain, and who had later accompanied a Geological Survey into the Barrens. He was friendly, in a treacherous sort of way,

66 Yet his time came, in the end, in the form of a little weazened man who spat broken English and many strange and uncouth exclamations. 99

smiling into one's face the while he meditated some underhand trick, as, for instance, when he stole from Buck's food at the first meal. As Buck sprang to punish him, the lash of François's whip sang through the air, reaching the culprit first; and nothing remained to Buck but to recover the bone. That was fair of François, he decided, and the half-breed began to rise in Buck's estimation.

The other dog made no advances, nor received any; also, he did not attempt to steal from the newcomers. He was a gloomy, morose fellow, and he showed Curly plainly that all he

The Siberian husky is used as a sled dog by the Eskimos and other Arctic natives, as well as the peoples of eastern Siberia. In the polar regions, humans cannot do without the help of this powerful animal, which can endure extremely low temperatures.

desired was to be left alone, and further, that there would be trouble if he were not left alone. "Dave" he was called, and he ate and slept, or yawned between times, and took interest in nothing, not even when the *Narwhal* crossed Queen Charlotte Sound and rolled and pitched and bucked like a thing possessed. When Buck and Curly grew excited, half wild with fear, he raised his head as though annoyed, favored them with an incurious glance, yawned, and went to sleep again.

66 One of them was a big, snow-white fellow from Spitzbergen who had been brought away by a whaling captain. He was friendly, in a treacherous sort of way, smiling into one's face the while he meditated some underhand trick. **99**

Miners leaving from Vancouver in 1898. This port in British Columbia (a Canadian province since 1875) profited from the boom in the Klondike, which lies in Canadian territory. The boats are bursting with bundle-toting passengers who are scarcely equipped for the cold—the Klondike's climate is a far cry from California's!

Day and night the ship throbbed to the tireless pulse of the propeller, and though one day was very like another, it was apparent to Buck that the weather was steadily growing colder. At last, one morning, the propeller was quiet, and the *Narwhal* was pervaded with an atmosphere of excitement. He felt it, as did the other dogs, and knew that a change was at hand. François leashed them and brought them on deck. At the first step upon the cold surface, Buck's feet sank into a white mushy something very like mud. He sprang back with a snort. More of this white stuff was falling through the air. He shook himself, but more of it fell upon him. He sniffed it curiously, then licked some up on his tongue. It bit like fire, and the next instant was gone. This puzzled him. He tried it again, with the same result. The onlookers laughed uproariously, and he felt ashamed, he knew not why, for it was his first snow.

66 At last, one morning, the propeller was quiet, and the *Narwhal* was pervaded with an atmosphere of excitement. **99**

2

THE LAW OF CLUB AND FANG

Buck's first day on the Dyea beach was like a nightmare. Every hour was filled with shock and surprise. He had been suddenly jerked from the heart of civilization and flung into the heart of things primordial. No lazy, sunkissed life was this, with nothing to do but loaf and be bored. Here was neither peace, nor rest, nor a moment's safety. All was confusion and action, and every moment life and limb were in peril. There was imperative need to be constantly alert; for these dogs and men were not town dogs and men. They were savages, all of them; who knew no law but the law of club and fang.

He had never seen dogs fight as these wolfish creatures fought, and his first experience taught him an unforgettable lesson. It is true, it was a vicarious experience, else he would not have lived to profit by it. Curly was the victim. They were camped near the log store, where she, in her friendly way, made advances to a husky dog the size of a full-grown wolf, though not half so large as she. There was no warning, only a leap in like a flash, a metallic clip of teeth, a leap out equally swift, and

25

In summer, on the tundra or in the taiga, huskies carry on their backs the tents and household objects of the Eskimos and Indians; in winter, six dogs are harnessed to a sled. Each team has a leader—the smartest and liveliest dog, feared and respected by its mates—which makes its fellow dogs obey their master's orders. To keep its place, the leader has to fight, at times even to the death (*above*). But the husky is more than a pack animal. Its keen sense of smell enables it to track for itself and its master the seals it feeds on.

Curly's face was ripped open from eye to jaw.

It was the wolf manner of fighting, to strike and leap away; but there was more to it than this. Thirty or forty huskies ran to the spot and surrounded the combatants in an intent and silent circle. Buck did not comprehend that silent intentness, nor the eager way with which they were licking their chops. Curly rushed her antagonist, who struck again and leaped aside. He met her next rush with his chest, in a peculiar fashion that tumbled her off her feet. She never regained them. This was what the onlooking huskies had waited for. They closed in upon her, snarling and yelping, and she was buried, screaming with agony, beneath the bristling mass of bodies.

So sudden was it, and so unexpected, that Buck was taken aback. He saw Spitz run out his scarlet tongue in a way he had of laughing; and he saw François swinging an axe, spring into the mess of dogs. Three men with clubs were helping him to scatter them. It did not take long. Two minutes from the time Curly went down, the last of her assailants were clubbed off. But she lay there limp and lifeless in the bloody, trampled snow, almost literally torn to pieces, the swart half-breed standing over her and cursing horribly. The scene often came back to Buck to trouble him in his sleep. So that was the way. No fair play. Once down, that was the end of you. Well, he would see to it that he never went down. Spitz ran out his tongue and laughed again and from that moment Buck hated him with a bitter and deathless hatred.

Before he had recovered from the shock caused by the tragic passing of Curly, he received another shock. François fastened upon him an arrangement of straps and buckles. It was a harness, such as he had seen the grooms put on the horses at home. And as he had seen horses work, so he was set to work, hauling François on a sled to the forest that fringed the valley, and returning with a load of firewood. Though his dignity was sorely hurt by thus being made a draught animal, he was too wise to rebel. He buckled down with a will and did his best, though it was all new and strange. François was stern, demanding instant obedience; and by virtue of his whip receiving instant obedience; while Dave, who was an experienced wheeler,

nipped Buck's hindquarters whenever he was in error. Spitz was the leader, likewise experienced, and while he could not always get at Buck, he growled sharp reproof now and again, or cunningly threw his weight in the traces to jerk Buck into the way he should go. Buck learned easily, and under the combined tuition of his two mates and François made remarkable progress. Ere they returned to camp he knew enough to stop at "ho," to go ahead at "mush," to swing wide on the bends; and to keep clear of the wheeler when the loaded sled shot downhill at their heels.

"T'ree vair' good dogs," François told Perrault. "Dat Buck, heem pool lak hell, I tich heem queek as anyt'ing."

By afternoon, Perrault, who was in a hurry to be on the trail with his dispatches, returned with two more dogs. "Billee" and "Joe" he called them, two brothers, and true huskies both. Sons of the one mother though they were, they were as different as day and night. Billee's one fault was his excessive good nature, while Joe was the very opposite, sour and introspective, with a perpetual snarl and a malignant eye. Buck received them in comradely fashion. Dave ignored them; while Spitz proceeded to thrash first one and then the other. Billee wagged his tail appeasingly, turned to run when he saw that appeasement was of no avail, and cried (still appeasingly) when Spitz's sharp teeth scored his flank. But no matter how Spitz circled, Joe whirled around on his heels to face him, mane bristling, ears laid back, lips writhing and snarling, jaws clipping together as fast as he could snap, and eyes diabolically

66 François fastened upon him an arrangement of straps and buckles. 99

In winter, the sled—or, to use the Algonquin Indian's term, *toboggan*—was the only means of efficient locomotion in the subarctic region. The native peoples invented sleds with a single crosspiece separated from the ground by two runners. The best sleds—highly prized in the Klondike—were made of wood; light and sturdy, they could support loads of up to 500 or even 700 pounds (200 to 300 kilograms). But the scarcity of this material in the tundra sometimes forced toboggan-makers to use whalebone for the runners and caribou antlers for the crosspieces.

Today, the husky is a highly valued pet. Its bright-eyed wolf's face, silken coat, lofty bearing, and gentleness make it a favorite companion for walking and athletics, including husky races. But while the people of the Arctic recognize the exceptional qualities of this breed, they very rarely make pets of them and, knowing that in the event of famine the dogs may end up as a meal, do not become attached to them.

66 Perrault secured another dog, an old husky, with a battle-scarred face and a single eye. 99

gleaming—the incarnation of belligerent fear. So terrible was his appearance that Spitz was forced to forego disciplining him; but to cover his own discomfiture he turned upon the inoffensive and wailing Billee and drove him to the confines of the camp.

By evening Perrault secured another dog, an old husky, long and lean and gaunt, with a battle-scarred face and a single eye which flashed a warning of prowess that commanded respect. He was called Sol-leks, which means the Angry One. Like

Dave, he asked nothing, gave nothing, expected nothing; and when he marched slowly and deliberately into their midst, even Spitz left him alone. He had one peculiarity which Buck was unlucky enough to discover. He did not like to be approached on his blind side. Of this offence Buck was unwittingly guilty, and the first knowledge he had of his indiscretion was when Sol-leks whirled upon him and slashed his shoulder to the bone for three inches up and down. Forever after Buck avoided his blind side, and to the last of their comradeship had no more trouble. His only apparent ambition, like Dave's, was to be left alone; though, as Buck was afterward to learn, each of them possessed one other and even more vital ambition.

That night Buck faced the great problem of sleeping. The

tent, illumined by a candle, glowed warmly in the midst of the white plain; and when he, as a matter of course, entered it, both Perrault and François bombarded him with curses and cooking utensils till he recovered from his consternation and fled ignominiously into the outer cold. A chill wind was blowing that nipped him sharply and bit with especial venom into his wounded shoulder. He lay down on the snow and attempted to sleep, but the frost soon drove him shivering to his feet. Miserable and disconsolate, he wandered about among the many tents, only to find that one place was as cold as another. Here and there savage dogs rushed upon him, but he bristled his neck-hair and snarled (for he was learning fast), and they let him go his way unmolested.

Finally an idea came to him. He would return and see how his own team-mates were making out. To his astonishment, they had disappeared. Again he wandered about through the great camp, looking for them, and again he returned. Were they in the tent? No, that could not be, else he would not have been driven out. Then where could they possibly be? With dropping tail and shivering body, very forlorn indeed, he aimlessly circled the tent. Suddenly the snow gave way beneath his fore legs and he sank down. Something wriggled under his feet. He sprang back, bristling and snarling, fearful of the unseen and unknown. But a friendly little yelp reassured him, and he went back to investigate. A whiff of warm air ascended to his nostrils, and there, curled up under the snow in a snug ball, lay Billee. He whined placatingly,

Lying down in the cold of a blizzard, this husky blankets itself in a protective layer of snow. In the morning, it will shake itself off and become its resilient self again, gobbling down its meat ration. Because of its remarkable resistance to low temperatures, the husky was transplanted from the North to the South Pole in the 1898–1900 expedition of Roald Amundsen and Robert Scott, the first explorers of the Antarctic continent; they owe part of their success to this exceptional dog.

66 Perrault and François bombarded him with curses and cooking utensils till he recovered from his consternation and fled ignominiously into the outer cold. 99

On Chilkoot Pass

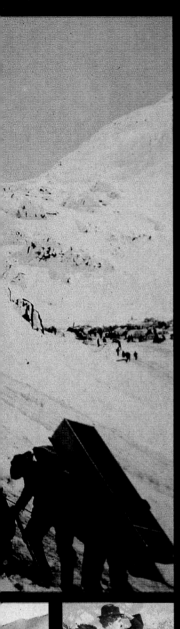

The Chilkoot Pass

From the shores of Dyea and Skagway, there are two routes toward Dawson City, the heart of the gold basin, and the fabled Klondike, a region named for the river running through it. The first route is the White Pass. At first access here looks easy—the pass is low, the trail passes over hills—but farther on there are chasms and riverbeds to cross; in autumn the trail turns into a river of mud; in winter it's a virtual skating rink. The second route climbs to the Chilkoot Pass at a height of over 3,282 feet (1,000 meters), on a glacial, windswept trail that the 25,000 people who climbed it made legendary. At the foot of the pass, the Canadian Mounted Police required every newcomer to bring along a year's worth of supplies. Some gave up, others lingered trying to get these supplies, only to be duped by con men. Others began the climb, carrying part of their supplies. Once at the top, they had no choice but to climb back down and brave the wearying ascent again until they amassed all they needed. This process could last as long as three months. In 1925 Charlie Chaplin's film *The Gold Rush* immortalized this "climb to hell."

In very fierce blizzards, the temperature can fall below -62 degrees Fahrenheit (-50 degrees Celsius), and there is a risk the dogs may die of cold. But their resilience depends on the quality of their nutrition. Every workday the husky receives a pound and a half (700 grams) of seal meat or pemmican, a mixture of dried beef, moose, or caribou meat combined with fat and wild berries.

squirmed and wriggled to show his good will and intention, and even ventured, as a bribe for peace, to lick Buck's face with his warm wet tongue.

Another lesson. So that was the way they did it, eh? Buck confidently selected a spot, and with much fuss and waste effort proceeded to dig a hole for himself. In a trice the heat from his body filled the confined space and he was asleep. The day had been long and arduous, and he slept soundly and comfortably, though he growled and barked and wrestled with bad dreams.

Nor did he open his eyes till roused by the noises of the waking camp. At first he did not know where he was. It had snowed during the night and he was completely buried. The snow walls pressed him on every side, and a great surge of fear swept through him—the fear of the wild thing for the trap. It was a token that he was harking back through his own life to the lives of his forebears; for he was a civilized dog, an unduly civilized dog, and of his own experience knew no trap and so could not of himself fear it. The muscles of his whole body contracted spasmodically and instinctively, the hair on his neck and shoulders stood on end, and with a ferocious snarl he bounded straight up into the blinding day, the snow flying about him in a flashing cloud. Ere he landed on his feet, he saw the white camp spread out before him and knew where he was and remembered all that had passed from the time he went for a stroll with Manuel to the hole he had dug for himself the night before.

A shout from François hailed his appearance. "Wot I say?" the dog-driver cried to Perrault. "Dat Buck for sure learn queek as anyt'ing."

Perrault nodded gravely. As courier for the Canadian Government, bearing important dispatches, he was anxious to secure the best dogs, and he was particularly gladdened by the possession of Buck.

Three more huskies were added to the team inside an hour, making a total of nine, and before another quarter of an hour had passed they were in harness and swinging up the trail toward the Dyea Cañon. Buck was glad to be gone, and though the work was hard he found he did not particularly despise it. He was surprised at the eagerness which animated the whole team

6 6 With a ferocious
snarl he bounded
straight up into the
blinding day, the snow
flying about him in a
flashing cloud. **9 9**

and which was communicated to him; but still more surprising was the change wrought in Dave and Sol-leks. They were new dogs, utterly transformed by the harness. All passiveness and unconcern had dropped from them. They were alert and active, anxious that the work should go well and fiercely irritable with whatever, by delay or confusion, retarded that work. The toil of the traces seemed the supreme expression of their being, and all that they lived for and the only thing in which they took delight.

Dave was wheeler or sled dog, pulling in front of him was Buck, then came Sol-leks; the rest of the team was strung out ahead, single file, to the leader, which position was filled by Spitz.

Buck had been purposely placed between Dave and Sol-leks so that he might receive instruction. Apt scholar that he was, they were equally apt teachers, never allowing him to linger long in error, and enforcing their teaching with sharp teeth. Dave was fair and very wise. He never nipped Buck without cause, and he never failed to nip him when he stood in need of it. As François's whip backed him up, Buck found it to be cheaper to mend his ways than to retaliate. Once, during a brief halt, when he got tangled in the traces and delayed the start, both Dave and Sol-leks flew at him and administered a sound trouncing. The resulting tangle was even worse; but Buck took good care to keep the traces clear thereafter; and ere the day was done, so well had he mastered his work, his mates about ceased nagging him. François's whip snapped less frequently, and Perrault even hon-

The Klondike is patrolled by the Canadian Mounted Police. Created to inspect the vast territory of the Canadian Northwest on horseback and to impress the Indians with their red jackets, at the end of the nineteenth century the Mounties also had to monitor a border invaded by miners.

ored Buck by lifting up his feet and carefully examining them.

It was a hard day's run, up the Cañon, through Sheep Camp, past the Scales and the timber line, across the glaciers and snow-drifts hundreds of feet deep, and over the great Chilcoot Divide, which stands between the salt water and the fresh, and guards forbiddingly the sad and lonely North. They made good time down the chain of lakes which fills the craters of extinct volcanoes, and late that night pulled into the huge camp at the head of Lake Bennett, where thousands of gold-seekers were building boats against the break-up of the ice in the spring. Buck made his hole in the snow and slept the sleep of the exhausted just, but all too early was routed out in the cold darkness and harnessed with his mates to the sled.

That day they made forty miles, the trail being packed; but the next day, and for many days to follow, they broke their own trail, worked harder, and made poorer time. As a rule, Perrault traveled ahead of the team, packing the snow with webbed shoes to make it easier for them. François, guiding the sled at the gee-pole, sometimes exchanged places with him, but

❝ It was a hard day's run. ❞

not often. Perrault was in a hurry, and he prided himself on his knowledge of ice, which knowledge was indispensable, for the fall ice was very thin, and where there was swift water, there was no ice at all.

Day after day, for days unending, Buck toiled in the traces. Always they broke camp in the dark, and the first grey of dawn found them hitting the trail with fresh miles reeled off behind them. And always they pitched camp after dark, eating their bit of fish, and crawling to sleep into the snow. Buck was ravenous. The pound and a half of sun-dried salmon, which was his ration for each day, seemed to go nowhere. He never had enough, and suffered from perpetual hunger pangs. Yet the other dogs, because they weighed less and were born to the life, received a pound only of the fish and managed to keep in good condition.

He swiftly lost the fastidiousness which had characterized his old life. A dainty eater, he found that his mates, finishing first, robbed him of his unfinished ration. There was no defending it. While he was fighting off two or three, it was disappearing down the throats of the others. To remedy this, he ate as fast

Once the *cheechakos* (Indian for "tenderfoot") crossed the Chilkoot Pass, his journey continued. But winter always halted it: the temperature approaches -40 degrees Fahrenheit, at times falling to -58 degrees (-30 to -60 degrees Celsius), preventing any work. Miners sheltered at Dawson City waiting for the thaw. On May 29, 1898, 30,000 fortune hunters embarked from Dawson City for the Yukon in 7,000 boats.

The husky has keen hunting instincts, which the Indians exploit for tracking animals. Left to its own devices, the dog will capture game and haul salmon from the fish-laden streams.

as they; and, so greatly did hunger compel him, he was not above taking what did not belong to him. He watched and learned. When he saw Pike, one of the new dogs, a clever malingerer and thief, slyly steal a slice of bacon when Perrault's back was turned, he duplicated the performance the following day, getting away with the whole chunk. A great uproar was raised, but he was unsuspected; while Dub, an awkward blunderer who was always getting caught, was punished for Buck's misdeed.

This first theft marked Buck as fit to survive in the hostile Northland environment. It marked his adaptability, his capacity to adjust himself to changing conditions, the lack of which would have meant swift and terrible death. It marked further decay or going to pieces of his moral nature, a vain thing and a handicap in the ruthless struggle for existence. It was all well enough in the Southland, under

the law of love and fellowship, to respect private property and personal feelings; but in the Northland, under the law of club and fang, who so took such things into account was a fool, and in so far as he observed them he would fail to prosper.

Not that Buck reasoned it out. He was fit, that was all, and unconsciously he accommodated himself to the new mode of life. All his days, no matter what the odds, he had never run from a fight. But the club of the man in the red sweater had beaten into him a more fundamental and primitive code. Civilized, he could have died for a moral consideration, say the defense of Judge Miller's riding-whip; but the completeness of his decivilization was not evidenced by his ability to flee from the defense of a moral consideration and so save his hide. He did not steal for joy of it but because of the clamor of his stomach. He did not rob openly, but stole secretly and cunningly, out of respect for club and fang. In short, the things he did were done because it was easier to do them than not to do them.

His development (or retrogression) was rapid. His muscles became hard as iron, and he grew callous to all ordinary pain. He achieved an internal as well as external economy. He could eat anything, no matter how loathsome or indigestible; and, once eaten, the juices of his stomach extracted the last least particle of nutriment; and his blood carried it to the farthest reaches of his body, building it into the toughest and stoutest of tissues. Sight and scent became remarkably keen, while his hearing developed such acuteness that in his sleep he heard the faintest sound and knew whether it heralded peace or peril. He learned to bite the ice out with his teeth when it collected between his toes; and when he was thirsty and there was a thick

66 Day after day, for days unending, Buck toiled in the traces.**99**

Rarely, even in the good weather, did the miners use horses, which are expensive to buy. Many, in fact, could not even afford to keep a team of dogs; instead they used human porters. Poorly fed themselves, those miners who did have a team cared little about the dogs' food supplies, forcing them to subsist on canned beef, leftover game, or even bean soup.

> 66 It was no task for him to learn to fight with cut and slash and the quick wolf snap. 99

scum of ice over the water hole, he would break it by rearing and striking it with stiff fore legs. His most conspicuous trait was an ability to scent the wind and forecast it a night in advance. No matter how breathless the air when he dug his nest by tree or bank, the wind that later blew inevitably found him to leeward, sheltered and snug.

And not only did he learn by experience, but instincts long dead became alive again. The domesticated generations fell from him. In vague ways he remembered back to the youth of the breed, to the time the wild dogs ranged in packs through the primeval forest and killed their meat as they ran it down. It was no task for him to learn to fight with cut and slash and the quick wolf snap. In this manner had fought forgotten ancestors. They quickened the old life within him, and the old tricks which they had stamped into the heredity of the breed were his tricks. They came to him without effort or discovery, as though they had been his always. And when, on the still cold nights, he pointed his nose at a star and howled long and wolflike, it was his ancestors, dead and dust, pointing nose at star and howling down through the centuries and through him. And his cadences were their cadences, the cadences which voiced their woe and what to them was the meaning of the stillness, and the cold, and dark.

Thus, as token of what a puppet thing life is, the ancient song surged through him and he came into his own again; and he came because men had found a yellow metal in the North, and because Manuel was a gardener's helper whose wages did not lap over the needs of his wife and divers small copies of himself which he had managed to accumulate.

Dogfights often break out, either because one of the team contests the dominance of the leader, or simply out of latent animal aggression. Every dog is therefore kept harnessed with a teammate, and the draught team's makeup changes only when an animal perishes. The size or sex of the dogs barely affects the quality of the team: a smaller female is just as resilient as a powerful male. The leader may even be female.

3

THE DOMINANT PRIMORDIAL BEAST

66 At the end of this day they made a bleak and miserable camp on the shore of Lake Le Barge. 99

The dominant primordial beast was strong in Buck, and under the fierce conditions of trail life it grew and grew. Yet it was a secret growth. His new-born cunning gave him poise and control. He was too busy adjusting himself to the new life to feel at ease, and not only did he not pick fights, but he avoided them whenever possible. A certain deliberateness characterized his attitude. He was not prone to rashness and precipitate action; and in the bitter hatred between him and Spitz he betrayed no impatience, shunned all offensive acts.

On the other hand, possibly because he divined in Buck a dangerous rival, Spitz never lost an opportunity of showing his teeth. He even went out of his way to bully Buck, striving constantly to start the fight which could end only in the death of one or the other. Early in the trip this might have taken place had it not been for an unwonted accident. At the end of this day they made a bleak and miserable camp on the shore of Lake Le Barge. Driving snow, a wind that cut like a white-hot knife, and darkness had forced them to grope for a camping place. They could hardly have fared worse. At their backs rose a perpendicular wall of rock, and Perrault and François were compelled to make their fire and spread their sleeping robes on the ice of the lake itself. The tent they had discarded at Dyea in

❝ Close in under the sheltering rock Buck made his nest. **❞**

The gold rush also drew Indians to Dawson City, Skagway, and Dyea, where they hired themselves out as guides or porters to miners without dogs or horses. The indigenous people of the Northwest are used to long marches; with leather straps across their brows, they can carry bundles of goods weighing as much as 65 pounds (30 kilograms).

order to travel light. A few sticks of driftwood furnished them with a fire that thawed down through the ice and left them to eat supper in the dark.

Close in under the sheltering rock Buck made his nest. So snug and warm was it, that he was loath to leave it when François distributed the fish which he had first thawed over the fire. But when Buck finished his ration and returned, he found his nest occupied. A warning snarl told him that his trespasser was Spitz. Till now Buck had avoided trouble with his enemy, but this was too much. The beast in him roared. He sprang upon Spitz with a fury which surprised them both, and Spitz particularly, for his whole experience with Buck had gone to teach him that his rival was an unusually timid dog, who managed to hold his own because of his great weight and size.

François was surprised, too, when they shot out in a tangle from the disrupted nest and he divined the cause of the trouble. "A-a-ah!" he cried to Buck. "Gif it to heem, by Gar! Gif it to heem, the dirty t'eef!"

Spitz was equally willing. He was crying with sheer rage and eagerness as he circled back and forth for a chance to spring in. Buck was no less eager, and no less cautious, as he likewise circled back and forth for the advantage. But it was then that the unexpected happened, the thing which projected their struggle for supremacy far

into the future, past many a weary mile of trail and toil.

An oath from Perrault, the resounding impact of a club upon a bony frame, and a shrill yelp of pain, heralded the breaking forth of pandemonium. The camp was suddenly discovered to be alive with skulking furry forms—starving huskies, four or five score of them, who had scented the camp from some Indian village. They had crept in while Buck and Spitz were fighting, and when the two men sprang among them with stout clubs they showed their teeth and fought back. They were crazed by the smell of the food. Perrault found one with head buried in the grub-box. His club landed heavily on the gaunt ribs, and the grub-box was capsized on the ground. On the instant a score of the famished brutes were scrambling for the bread and bacon. The clubs fell upon them unheeded. They yelped and howled under the rain of blows, but struggled none the less madly till the last crumb had been devoured.

In the meantime the astonished team-dogs had burst out of their nests only to be set upon by the fierce invaders. Never had Buck seen such dogs. It seemed as though their bones would burst through their skins. They were mere skeletons, draped loosely in draggled hides, with blazing eyes and slavered fangs. But the hunger-madness made them terrifying, irresistible. There was no opposing them. The team-dogs were swept back against the cliff at the first onset. Buck was beset by three huskies, and in a trice his head and shoulders were ripped and slashed. The din was frightful. Billee was crying as usual. Dave and Sol-leks, dripping blood from a score of wounds, were fighting bravely side by side. Joe was snapping like a demon. Once, his teeth closed on the foreleg of a husky, and he crunched down through the bone. Pike, the malingerer, leaped upon the crippled animal, breaking its neck with a quick flash of teeth and a jerk. Buck got a frothing adversary by the throat, and was sprayed with blood when his teeth sank through the jugular. The warm taste of it in his mouth goaded him to greater fierceness. He flung himself upon another, and at the same time felt teeth sink in his own throat. It was Spitz, treacherously attacking from the side.

Perrault and François, having cleaned out their part of the camp, hurried to save their sled-dogs. The wild wave of famished beasts rolled back before them, and Buck shook himself free. But

The Klondike, like all of the late nineteenth-century American Northwest, had a wide variety of animal life, dominated by predators. The two larger tracks shown below belong to the wolf, which has not been exterminated there as it has in Europe and much of the rest of the American continent; the two smaller tracks are those of the fox, which is much sought after for its fur, particularly the silver fox.

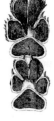
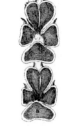

At night, the native Arctic people run a line from their dogs to a tree or a whale rib planted in the ice. Let loose, the animals would run away and join a wolf pack.

66 The hunger-madness made them terrifying, irrestible. 99

it was only for a moment. The two men were compelled to run back to save the grub, upon which the huskies returned to the attack on the team. Billee, terrified into bravery, sprang through the savage circle and fled away over the ice. Pike and Dub followed on his heels, with the rest of the team behind. As Buck drew himself together to spring after them, out of the tail of his eye he saw Spitz rush upon him with the evident intention of overthrowing him. Once off his feet and under that mass of huskies, there was no hope for him. But he braced himself to the shock of Spitz's charge, then joined the flight out on the lake. ✳

Later, the nine team-dogs gathered together and sought shelter in the forest. Though unpursued, they were in a sorry plight. There was not one who was not wounded in four or five places, while some were wounded grievously. Dub was badly injured in a hind leg; Dolly, the last husky added to the team at Dyea, had a badly torn throat; Joe had lost an eye; while Billee, the good-natured, with an ear chewed and rent to ribbons, cried and whimpered throughout the night. At daybreak they limped warily back to camp, to find the marauders gone and the two men in bad tempers. Fully half their grub supply was gone. The huskies had chewed through the sled lashings and canvas coverings. In fact, nothing, no matter how remotely eatable, had escaped them. They had eaten a pair of Perrault's moose-hide moccasins, chunks out of the leather traces, and even two feet of lash from the end of François's whip. He broke from a mournful contemplation of it to look over his wounded dogs.

"Ah, my frien's," he said softly, "mebbe it mek you mad dog, dose many bites. Mebbe all mad dog, sacredam! Wot you t'ink, eh, Perrault?"

The courier shook his head dubiously. With four hundred miles of trail still between him and Dawson, he could ill afford to have madness break out among his dogs. Two hours of cursing and exertion got the harness into shape, and the wound-stiffened team was under way, struggling painfully over the hardest part of the trail they had yet encountered, and for that matter, the hardest between them and Dawson.

The Thirty Mile River was wide open. Its wild water defied the frost, and it was in the eddies only and in the quiet places that the ice held at all. Six days of exhausting toil were required to cover those thirty terrible miles. And terrible they were, for every foot of them was accomplished at the risk of life to dog and man. A dozen times, Perrault, nosing the way, broke through the ice bridges, being saved by the long pole he carried, which he so held that it fell each time across the hole made by his body. But a cold snap was on, the thermometer registering fifty below zero, and

66 A dozen times, Perrault broke through the ice bridges, being saved by the long pole he carried. 99

66 Each time he broke through he was compelled for very life to build a fire and dry his garments. 99

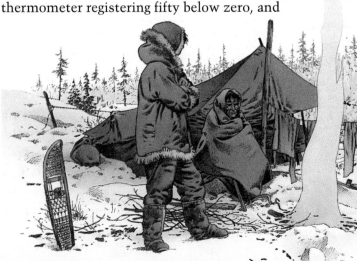

43

each time he broke through he was compelled for very life to build a fire and dry his garments.

Nothing daunted him. It was because nothing daunted him that he had been chosen for government courier. He took all manner of risks, resolutely thrusting his little weazened face into the frost and struggling on from dim dawn to dark. He skirted the frowning shores on rim ice that bent and crackled under foot and upon which they dared not halt. Once, the sled broke through, with Dave and Buck, and they were half-frozen and all but drowned by the time they were dragged out. The usual fire was necessary to save them. They were coated solidly with ice, and the two men kept them on the run around the fire, sweating and thawing, so close that they were singed by the flames.

At another time Spitz went through, dragging the whole team after him up to Buck, who strained backward with all his strength, his forepaws on the slippery edge and the ice quivering and snapping all around. But behind him was Dave, likewise straining backward, and behind the sled was François, pulling till his tendons cracked.

Again the rim ice broke away before and behind, and there was no escape except up the cliff. Perrault scaled it by a miracle, while François prayed for just that miracle; and with every thong and sled lashing and the last bit of harness rove into a long rope, the dogs were hoisted, one by one, to the cliff crest. François came up last, after the sled and load. Then came the search for a place to descend, which descent was ultimately made by the aid of the rope, and night found them back on the river with a quarter of a mile to the day's credit.

By the time they made the Hootalinqua and good ice, Buck was played out. The rest of the dogs were in like condition; but Perrault, to make up lost time, pushed them late and early. The first day they covered thirty-five miles to the Big Salmon; the next day thirty-five more to the Little Salmon; the third day forty miles, which brought them well up towards the Five Fingers.

Buck's feet were not so compact and hard as the feet of the huskies. His had softened during the many

66 François came up last, after the sled and load. 99

generations since the day his last wild ancestor was tamed by a cave-dweller or river man. All day long he limped in agony, and camp once made, lay down like a dead dog. Hungry as he was, he would not move to receive his ration of fish, which François had to bring to him. Also, the dog-driver rubbed Buck's feet for half an hour each night after supper, and sacrificed the tops of his own moccasins to make four moccasins for Buck. This was a great relief, and Buck caused even the weazened face of

66 The dog-driver sacrificed the tops of his own moccasins to make four moccasins for Buck. 99

Perrault to twist itself into a grin one morning, when François forgot the moccasins and Buck lay on his back, his four feet waving appealingly in the air, and refused to budge without them. Later his feet grew hard to the trail, and the worn-out foot-gear was thrown away.

At the Pelly one morning, as they were harnessing up, Dolly, who had never been conspicuous for anything, went suddenly mad. She announced her condition by a long, heart-breaking wolf howl that sent every dog bristling with fear, then sprang straight for Buck. He had never seen a dog go mad, nor did he have any reason to fear madness; yet he knew that here was horror, and fled away from it in a panic. Straight away he raced, with Dolly, panting and frothing, one leap behind; nor could she gain on him, so great was his terror, nor could he leave her, so great was her madness. He plunged through the wooded breast of the island, flew down to the lower end, crossed a back channel filled with rough ice to another island, gained a third island, curved back to the main river and in desperation started to cross it. And all the time, though he did not look, he could hear her snarling just one leap behind. François called to him a quarter of a mile away and he doubled back, still one leap ahead, gasping painfully for air and putting all his faith in that François would save him. The dog-driver held the axe poised in his hand, and as Buck shot past him the axe crashed down upon mad Dolly's head.

> **Straight away he raced, with Dolly, panting and frothing, one leap behind.**

Buck staggered over against the sled, exhausted, sobbing for breath, helpless. This was Spitz's opportunity. He sprang upon Buck, and twice his teeth sank into his unresisting foe and ripped and tore the flesh to the bone. Then François's lash descended, and Buck had the satisfaction of watching Spitz receive the worst whipping as yet administered to any of the team.

"One devil, dat Spitz," remarked Perrault. "Some dam day heem keel dat Buck."

"Dat Buck two devils," was François's rejoinder. "All de tam I watch dat Buck I know for sure. Lissen: some dam fine day heem get mad lak hell an' den heem chew dat Spitz all up an' spit heem out on de snow. Sure. I know."

From then on it was war between them. Spitz, as lead-dog and acknowledged master of the team, felt his supremacy threatened by this strange Southland dog. And strange Buck was to him, for of the many Southland dogs he had known, not one had shown up worthily in camp and on trail. They were all too soft, dying under the toil, the frost, and starvation. Buck was the exception. He alone endured and prospered, matching the husky in strength, savagery, and cunning. Then he was a masterful dog, and what made him dangerous was the fact that the club of the man in the red sweater had knocked all blind pluck and rashness out of his desire for mastery. He was pre-eminently cunning, and could bide his time with a patience that was nothing less than primitive.

It was inevitable that the clash for leadership should come. Buck wanted it. He wanted it because it was his nature, because he had been gripped tight by that nameless, incomprehensible pride of the trail and trace—that pride which holds dogs in the toil to the last gasp, which lures them to die joyfully in the harness, and breaks their hearts if they are cut out of the harness. This was the pride of Dave as wheel-dog, of Sol-leks as he pulled with all his strength; the pride that laid hold of them at break of camp, transforming them from sour and sullen brutes into straining, eager, ambitious creatures; the pride that spurred them on all day and dropped them at pitch of camp at night, letting them fall back into gloomy unrest and uncontent. This was the pride that bore up Spitz and made him thrash the sled-dogs who blundered and shirked in the traces or hid away at harness-up time in the morning. Likewise it was his pride that made him fear Buck as a possible lead-dog. And this was Buck's pride, too.

He openly threatened the other's leadership. He came between him and the shirks he should have punished. And he did it deliberately. One night there was a heavy snowfall, and in the morning Pike, the malingerer, did not appear. He was securely hidden in his nest under a foot of snow. François called him and sought him in vain. Spitz was wild with wrath. He raged through the camp, smelling and digging in every likely place, snarling so frightfully that Pike heard and shivered in his hiding-place.

But when he was at last unearthed, and Spitz flew at him to punish him, Buck flew, with equal rage, in between. So unexpected was it, and so shrewdly managed, that Spitz was hurled backward and off his feet. Pike, who had been trembling abjectly, took heart at this open mutiny, and sprang upon his overthrown leader. Buck, to whom fair play was a forgotten code, likewise sprang upon Spitz. But François, chuckling at the incident while unswerving in the administration of justice, brought his lash down upon Buck with all his might. This failed to drive Buck from his prostrate rival, and the butt of the whip was brought into play. Half-stunned by the blow, Buck was knocked backward and the lash laid upon him again and again,

The shape of dog harnesses varies by region. The Indians prefer fan-shaped team formations. In the West and the Klondike, the dogs are lined up in pairs.

47

Wolves live in packs which usually consist of five or six adults and as many young. The pack is led by a male and a female, who form the dominant couple. The pack's territory extends over more than seven square miles, sometimes even more. As a group, the wolves hunt herbivorous animals, almost invariably using one particular tactic: one or two wolves charge upon the herd to spread panic; the others watch for the weakest animals, and wait for the best moment to attack them.

while Spitz soundly punished the many times offending Pike.

In the days that followed, as Dawson grew closer and closer, Buck still continued to interfere between Spitz and the culprits; but he did it craftily, when François was not around. With the covert mutiny of Buck, a general insubordination sprang up and increased. Dave and Sol-leks were unaffected, but the rest of the team went from bad to worse. Things no longer went right. There was continual bickering and jangling. Trouble was always afoot, and at the bottom of it was Buck. He kept François busy, for the dog-driver was in constant apprehension of the life-and-death struggle between the two which he knew must take place sooner or later; and on more than one night the sounds of quarrelling and strife among the other dogs turned him out of his sleeping robe, fearful that Buck and Spitz were at it.

But the opportunity did not present itself, and they pulled into Dawson one dreary afternoon with the great fight still to come. Here were many men, and countless dogs, and Buck found them all at work. It seemed the ordained order of things that dogs should work. All day they swung up and down the main street in long teams, and in the night their jingling bells still went by. They hauled cabin logs and firewood, freighted up to the mines, and did all manner of work that horses did in the Santa Clara Valley. Here and there Buck met Southland dogs, but in the main they were the wild wolf husky breed. Every night, regularly at night, at twelve, at three, they lifted a nocturnal song, a weird and eerie, chant, in which it was Buck's delight to join.

With the aurora borealis flaming coldly overhead, or the stars leaping in the frost dance, and the land numb and frozen under its pall of snow, this song of the huskies might have been the defiance of life, only it was pitched in minor key, with long-drawn wailings and half-sobs, and was more the pleading of life, the articulate travail of existence. It was an old song, old as the breed itself – one of the first songs of the younger world in a day when songs were sad. It was invested with the woe of unnumbered generations, this plaint by which Buck was so strangely stirred. When he moaned and sobbed, it was with the pain of living that was of old the pain of his wild fathers, and the fear and mystery of the cold and dark that was to them fear and mystery. And that he should be stirred by it marked the

66 They pulled into Dawson. **99**

completeness with which he harked back through the ages of fire and roof to the raw beginnings of life in the howling ages.

Seven days from the time they pulled into Dawson, they dropped down the steep bank by the Barracks to the Yukon Trail, and pulled for Dyea and Salt Water. Perrault was carrying despatches if anything more urgent than those he had brought in; also, the travel pride had gripped him, and he purposed to make the record trip of the year. Several things favored him in this. The week's rest had recuperated the dogs and put them in thorough trim. The trail they had broken into the country was packed hard by later journeyers. And further, the police had arranged in two or three places deposits of grub for dog and man, and he was traveling light.

They made Sixty Mile, which is a fifty-mile run, on the first day; and the second day saw them booming up the Yukon well on their way to Pelly. But such splendid running was achieved not without great trouble and vexation on the part of François. The insidious revolt led by Buck had destroyed the solidarity of the team. It no longer was as one dog leaping in the

At night, muzzle pointed skyward, wolves howl to signal their presence, stake out their territory, or call other packs. Like other dogs, the husky still howls, and when hearing wolves, it will sometimes imitate their howl.

49

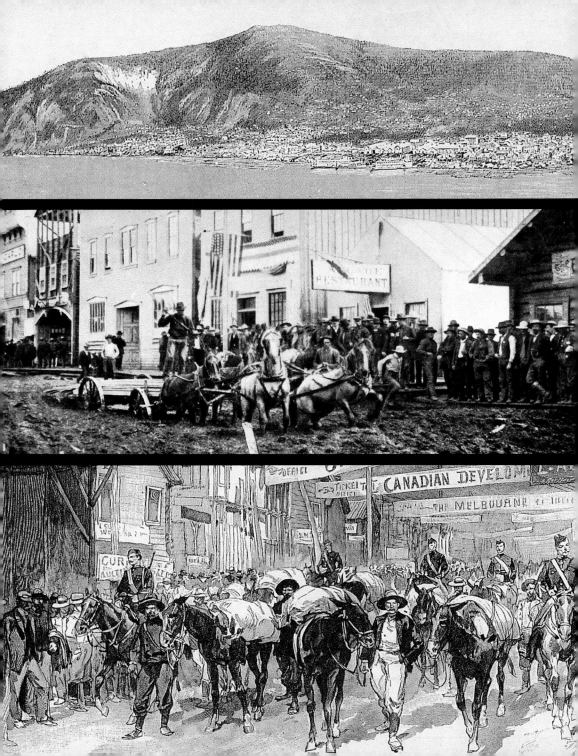

Dawson City

Situated where the Yukon and Klondike rivers meet, Dawson City (*top*) became the gold capital. A mere trading post before the gold rush of July 1898, the city became one of the largest in the Northwest in a matter of three weeks: several banks were built, five churches, a theater, and thirty saloons that offered the miners means to squander their earnings quickly. The cost of living and services quintupled in just a few months. A carpenter, a cook, or a bartender could earn a great deal of money. Even if the miners didn't strike it rich, at least the merchants were guaranteed profits. Bags of gold arrived with mounted police escort (*bottom left*) to accompany them to the bank vaults. This spectacular entrance roused the hopes and dreams of the whole population stranded in this outpost where, in summer, the streets became virtual mud pits in which men and beasts alike wallowed (*center left*). Dawson City was no haven for the down-and-out: the Mounted Police made every effort to convince them to leave a city whose supplies, brought by small steamboats going upriver, could not be assured in the long winter months.

Beginning in the summer of 1899, people came in droves to Dawson City. The mining concessions rose from 5,000 in January 1898 to 17,000 in July 1899. By this time, the best sites were snatched up and the veins were already depleted; many of the disappointed returned home ruined after having invested all their scant savings in supplies and survival. In August 1899, thousands of miners started to abandon the Klondike, passing one last time through Dawson City, where the party was still not over for a lucky few.

The health of sled dogs is a matter of care and concern to the driving crew, who inspect their paws and teeth on a daily basis.

traces. The encouragement Buck gave the rebels led them into all kinds of petty misdemeanors. No more was Spitz a leader greatly to be feared. The old awe departed, and they grew equal to challenging his authority. Pike robbed him of half a fish one night, and gulped it down under the protection of Buck. Another night Dub and Joe fought Spitz and made him forego the punishment they deserved. And even Billee, the good-natured, was less good-natured, and whined not half so placatingly as in former days. Buck never came near Spitz without snarling and bristling menacingly. In fact, his conduct approached that of a bully, and he was given to swaggering up and down before Spitz's very nose.

The breaking down of discipline likewise affected the dogs in their relations with one another. They quarreled and bickered more than ever among themselves, till at times the camp was a howling bedlam. Dave and Sol-leks alone were unaltered, though they were made irritable by the unending squabbling. François swore strange barbarous oaths, and stamped the snow in futile rage, and tore his hair. His lash was always singing among the dogs, but it was of small avail. Directly his back was turned they were at it again. He backed up Spitz with his whip, while Buck backed up the remainder of the team. François knew he was behind all the trouble, and Buck knew he knew; but Buck was too clever ever again to be caught red-handed. He worked faithfully in the harness, for the toil had become a delight to him; yet it was a greater delight slyly to precipitate a fight amongst his mates and tangle the traces.

At the mouth of the Tahkeena, one night after supper, Dub turned up a snowshoe rabbit, blundered it, and missed. In a second the whole team was in full cry. A hundred yards away was a camp of the Northwest Police, with fifty dogs, huskies all, who joined the chase. The rabbit sped down the river, turned off into a small creek, up the frozen bed of which it held steadily. It ran lightly on the surface of the snow, while the dogs ploughed

through by main strength. Buck led the pack, sixty strong, around bend after bend, but he could not gain. He lay down low to the race, whining eagerly, his splendid body flashing for-

ward, leap by leap, in the wan white moonlight. And leap by leap, like some pale frost wraith, the snowshoe rabbit flashed on ahead.

All that stirring of old instincts which at stated periods drives men out from the sounding cities to forest and plain to kill things by chemically propelled leaden pellets, the blood lust, the joy to kill—all this was Buck's, only it was infinitely more intimate. He was ranging at the head of the pack, running the

wild thing down, the living meat, to kill with his own teeth and wash his muzzle to the eyes in warm blood.

There is an ecstasy that marks the summit of life, and beyond which life cannot rise. And such is the paradox of living, this ecstasy comes when one is most alive, and it comes as a complete forgetfulness that one is alive. This ecstasy, this forgetfulness of living, comes to the artist, caught up and out of himself in a sheet of flame; it comes to the soldier, war-mad on a stricken field and refusing quarter; and it came to Buck, leading the pack, sounding the old

The hare's prints mark a trail to its favorite grazing land. In winter, its fur turns white, helping it to elude all predators but its uncommonly sharp-eyed enemy the lynx.

wolf-cry, straining after the food that was alive and that fled swiftly before him through the moonlight. He was sounding the deeps of his nature, and of the parts of his nature that were deeper than he, going back into the womb of Time. He was mastered by the sheer surging of life, the tidal wave of being, the perfect joy of each separate muscle, joint, and sinew in that it was everything that was not death, that it was aglow and rampant, expressing itself in movement, flying exultantly under the stars and over the face of dead matter that did not move.

66 He was ranging at the head of the pack, running the wild thing down. **99**

But Spitz, cold and calculating even in his supreme moods, left the pack and cut across a narrow neck of land where the creek made a long bend around. Buck did not know of this, and as he rounded the bend, the frost

wraith of a rabbit still flitting before him, he saw another and larger frost wraith leap from the overhanging bank into the immediate path of the rabbit. It was Spitz. The rabbit could not turn, and as the white teeth broke its back in midair it shrieked as loudly as a stricken man may shriek. At sound of this, the cry of Life plunging down from Life's apex in the grip of Death, the full pack at Buck's heels raised a hell's chorus of delight.

Buck did not cry out. He did not check himself, but drove in upon Spitz, shoulder to shoulder, so hard that he missed the throat. They rolled over and over in the powdery snow. Spitz

Wolves communicate among themselves by howls, facial gestures, and stance. *Above,* the male leader of the pack, pricking up his ears and baring his teeth, asserts his authority.

66 In a flash Buck knew it. The time had come. It was to the death. **99**

gained his feet almost as though he had not been overthrown, slashing Buck down the shoulder and leaping clear. Twice his teeth clipped together, like the steel jaws of a trap, as he backed away for better footing, with lean and lifting lips that writhed and snarled.

In a flash Buck knew it. The time had come. It was to the death. As they circled about, snarling, ears laid back, keenly watchful for the advantage, the scene came to Buck with a sense of familiarity. He seemed to remember it all—the white woods, and earth, and moonlight, and the thrill of battle. Over the whiteness and silence brooded a ghostly calm. There was not the faintest whisper of air—nothing moved, not a leaf quivered, the visible breaths of the dogs rising slowly and lingering in the frosty air. They had made short work of the snowshoe rabbit, these dogs that were ill-tamed wolves; and they were now drawn up in an expectant circle. They, too, were silent, their eyes only

gleaming and their breaths drifting slowly upward. To Buck it was nothing new or strange, this scene of old time. It was as though it had always been the wonted way of things.

Spitz was a practiced fighter. From Spitzbergen through the Arctic, and across Canada and the Barrens, he had held his own with all manner of dogs and achieved to mastery over them. Bitter rage was his, but never blind rage. In passion to rend and destroy, he never forgot that his enemy was in like passion to rend and destroy. He never rushed till he was prepared to receive a rush; never attacked till he had first defended that attack.

In vain Buck strove to sink his teeth in the neck of the big white dog. Wherever his fangs struck for the softer flesh, they were countered by the fangs of Spitz. Fang clashed fang, and lips were cut and bleeding, but Buck could not penetrate his enemy's guard. Then he warmed up and enveloped Spitz in a whirlwind of rushes. Time and time again he tried for the snow-white throat, where life bubbled near to the surface, and each time and every time Spitz slashed him and got away. Then Buck took to rushing, as though for the throat, when, suddenly drawing back his head and curving in from the side, he would drive his shoulder at the shoulder of Spitz, as a ram by which to overthrow him. But instead, Buck's shoulder was slashed down each time as Spitz leaped lightly away.

❝ Spitz was a practiced fighter. **❞**

Spitz was untouched, while Buck was streaming with blood and panting hard. The fight was growing desperate. And all the while the silent and wolfish circle waited to finish off whichever dog went down. As Buck grew winded, Spitz took to rushing, and he kept him staggering for footing. Once Buck went over, and the whole circle of sixty dogs started up; but he recovered himself, almost in midair, and the circle sank down again and waited.

But Buck possessed a quality that made for greatness— imagination. He fought by instinct, but he could fight by head as well. He rushed, as though attempting the old shoulder trick, but at the last instant swept low to the snow and in. His teeth closed on Spitz's left foreleg. There was a crunch of breaking bone, and

Poised to attack, its mouth open wide, the wolf is a formidable adversary: its powerful jaws contain forty-two teeth, including four pointed canines that may grow to nearly 2 1/2 inches (6 centimeters) and are capable of piercing thick fur. Once it has sunk its fangs into something, the wolf does not let go.

the white dog faced him on three legs. Thrice he tried to knock him over, then repeated the trick and broke the right foreleg. Despite the pain and helplessness, Spitz struggled madly to keep up. He saw the silent circle, with gleaming eyes, lolling tongues, and silvery breaths drifting upward, closing in upon him as he had seen similar circles close in upon beaten antagonists in the past. Only this time he was the one who was beaten.

There was no hope for him. Buck was inexorable. Mercy was a thing reserved for gentler climes. He maneuvered for the final rush. The circle had tightened till he could feel the breaths

66 Despite the pain and helplessness, Spitz struggled madly to keep up. 99

of the huskies on his flanks. He could see them, beyond Spitz and to either side, half crouching for the spring, their eyes fixed upon him. A pause seemed to fall. Every animal was motionless as though turned to stone. Only Spitz quivered and bristled as he staggered back and forth, snarling with horrible menace, as though to frighten off impending death. Then Buck sprang in and out; but while he was in, shoulder had at last squarely met shoulder. The dark circle became a dot on the moon-flooded snow as Spitz disappeared from view. Buck stood and looked on, the successful champion, the dominant primordial beast who had made his kill and found it good.

4

WHO HAS WON TO MASTERSHIP

66 Buck took up the duties of leadership. 99

"Eh? Wot I say? I spik true w'en I say dat Buck two devils."

This was François's speech next morning when he discovered Spitz missing and Buck covered with wounds. He drew him to the fire and by its light pointed them out.

"Dat Spitz fight lak hell," said Perrault, as he surveyed the gaping rips and cuts.

"An' dat Buck fight lak two hells," was François's answer. "An' now we make good time. No more Spitz, no more trouble, sure."

While Perrault packed the camp outfit and loaded the sled, the dog-driver proceeded to harness the dogs. Buck trotted up to the place Spitz would have occupied as leader; but François, not noticing him, brought Sol-leks to the coveted position. In his judgement, Sol-leks was the best lead-dog left. Buck sprang upon Sol-leks in a fury, driving him back and standing in his place.

"Eh? eh?" François cried, slapping his thighs gleefully.

"Look at dat Buck. Heem keel dat Spitz, heem t'ink to take de job."

Wrapped up against the cold, a prospector dozes under a protective canopy.

"Go 'way, Chook!" he cried, but Buck refused to budge.

He took Buck by the scruff of the neck, and though the dog growled threateningly, dragged him to one side and replaced Sol-leks. The old dog did not like it, and showed plainly that he was afraid of Buck. François was obdurate, but when he turned his back Buck again displaced Sol-leks, who was not at all unwilling to go.

François was angry. "Now, by Gar, I feex you!" he cried, coming back with a heavy club in his hand.

Buck remembered the man in the red sweater, and retreated slowly; nor did he attempt to charge in when Sol-leks was once more brought forward. But he circled just beyond the range of the club, snarling with bitterness and rage; and while he circled he watched the club so as to dodge it if thrown by François, for he was become wise in the way of clubs.

66 François was angry. 'Now, by Gar, I feex you!' he cried, coming back with a heavy club in his hand. 99

The driver went about his work, and he called to Buck when he was ready to put him in his old place in front of Dave. Buck retreated two or three steps. François followed him up, whereupon he again retreated. After some time of this, François threw down his club, thinking that Buck feared a thrashing. But Buck was in open revolt. He wanted not to escape a clubbing but to have the leadership. It was his by right. He had earned it, and he would not be content with less.

A picnic in the snow: in the freezing open air, the men eat their plates of baked beans.

Perrault took a hand. Between them they ran him about for the better part of an hour. They threw clubs at him. He dodged. They cursed him, and his fathers and mothers before him, and all his seed to come after him down to the remotest generation, and every hair on his body and drop of blood in his veins; and he answered curse with snarl and

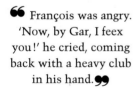

58

kept out of their reach. He did not try to run away, but retreated around and around the camp, advertising plainly that when his desire was met, he would come in and be good.

François sat down and scratched his head. Perrault looked at his watch and swore. Time was flying, and they should have been on the trail an hour gone. François scratched his head again. He shook it and grinned sheepishly at the courier, who shrugged his shoulders in sign that they were beaten. Then François went up to where Sol-leks stood and called to Buck. Buck laughed, as dogs laugh, yet kept his distance. François unfastened Sol-leks's traces and put him back in his old place. The team stood harnessed to the sled in an unbroken line, ready for the trail. There was no place for Buck save at the front. Once more François called, and once more Buck laughed and kept away.

"T'row down de club," Perrault commanded.

François complied, whereupon Buck trotted in, laughing triumphantly, and swung around into position at the head of the team. His traces were fastened, the sled broken out, and with both men running they dashed out on to the river trail.

Highly as the dog-driver had forevalued Buck, with his two devils, he found, while the day was yet young, that he had undervalued. At a bound Buck took up the duties of leadership; and where judgement was required, and quick thinking and quick acting, he showed himself the superior even of Spitz, of whom François had never seen an equal.

But it was in giving the law and making his mates live up to it, that Buck excelled. Dave and Sol-leks did not mind the change in leadership. It was none of their business. Their business was to toil, and toil mightily, in the traces. So long as that were not interfered with, they did not care what happened. Billee, the good-natured, could lead for all they cared so long as he kept order. The rest of the team, however, had grown unruly during the last days of Spitz, and their surprise was great now that Buck proceeded to lick them into shape.

Pike, who pulled at Buck's heels, and who never put an ounce more of his weight against the breast-band than he was compelled to do, was swiftly and repeatedly shaken for loafing; and ere the first day was done he was pulling more than ever

This sculpted ivory stopper made from a walrus tusk is used to hold sled reins in place. Because of the scarcity of wood in the tundra, the native arctic peoples carve walrus tusks instead to make functional objects as well as small statues representing mytho-logical figures.

before in his life. The first night in camp, Joe, the sour one, was punished roundly—a thing that Spitz had never succeeded in doing. Buck simply smothered him by virtue of superior weight, and cut him up till he ceased snapping and began to whine for mercy.

The general tone of the team picked up immediately. It recovered its old-time solidarity, and once more the dogs leaped as one dog in the traces. At the Rink Rapids two native huskies, Teek and Koona, were added; and the celerity with which Buck broke them in took François's breath.

"Nevaire such a dog as dat Buck!" he cried. "No, nevaire! Heem worth one t'ousan' dollair, by Gar! Eh? Wot you say, Perrault?"

And Perrault nodded. He was ahead of the record then, and gaining day by day. The trail was in excellent condition, well packed and hard, and there was no new-fallen snow with which

Throughout the winter, the prospectors made their way by following the paths of frozen rivers. Those who did not own animal teams pulled the supply sleds themselves. Horses, unable to travel in thick snow, are rarely used in this region.

to contend. It was not too cold. The temperature dropped to fifty below zero and remained there the whole trip. The men rode and ran by turn, and the dogs were kept on the jump, with but infrequent stoppages.

The Thirty Mile River was comparatively coated with ice, and they covered in one day going out what had taken them ten days coming in. In one run they made a sixty-mile dash from the foot of Lake Le Barge to the White Horse Rapids. Across Marsh, Tagish, and Bennet (seventy miles of lakes), they flew so fast that the man whose turn it was to run towed behind the sled at the end of a rope. And on the last night of the second week they topped White Pass and dropped down the sea slope with the lights of Skaguay and of the shipping at their feet.

It was a record run. Each day for fourteen days they had averaged forty miles. For three days Perrault and François threw chests up and down the main street of Skaguay and were deluged with invitations to drink, while the team was the constant center of a worshipful crowd of dog-busters and mushers. Then three or four western bad men aspired to clean out the town, were riddled like pepper-boxes for their pains, and public interest turned to other idols. Next came official orders. François called

Buck to him, threw his arms around him, wept over him. And that was the last of François and Perrault. Like other men, they passed out of Buck's life for good.

A Scotch half-breed took charge of him and his mates, and in company with a dozen other dog teams he started back over the weary trail to Dawson. It was no light running now, nor record time, but heavy toil each day, with a heavy load behind; for this was the mail train, carrying word from the world to the men who sought gold under the shadow of the Pole.

At the top of the White Pass, prospectors catch their breath before resuming their hard trek.

Buck did not like it, but he bore up well to the work, taking pride in it after the manner of Dave and Sol-leks, and seeing that his mates, whether they prided in it or not, did their fair share. It was a monotonous life, operating with machine-like regularity. One day was very like another. At a certain time each morning the cooks turned out, fires were built, and breakfast was eaten. Then, while some broke camp, others harnessed the dogs, and they were under way an hour or so before the darkness fell which gave warning of dawn. At night, camp was made. Some pitched the flies, others cut firewood and pine boughs for the beds, and still others carried water or ice for the cooks. Also, the dogs were fed. To them, this was the one feature of the day, though it was good to loaf around, after the fish was eaten, for an hour or so with the other dogs, of which there were fivescore and odd. There were fierce fighters among them, but three battles with the fiercest brought Buck to mastery, so that when he bristled and showed his teeth they got out of the way.

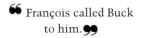

66 François called Buck to him. **99**

Best of all, perhaps, he loved to lie near the fire, hind legs crouched under him, forelegs stretched out in front, head raised, and eyes blinking dreamily at the flames. Sometimes he thought of Judge Miller's big house in the sun-kissed Santa Clara Valley, and of the cement swimming-

Most prospectors were bachelors or set out alone, although some risked bringing their families on the adventure. *Below*, a mining camp.

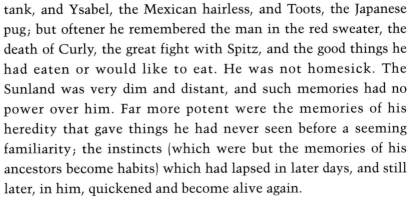

tank, and Ysabel, the Mexican hairless, and Toots, the Japanese pug; but oftener he remembered the man in the red sweater, the death of Curly, the great fight with Spitz, and the good things he had eaten or would like to eat. He was not homesick. The Sunland was very dim and distant, and such memories had no power over him. Far more potent were the memories of his heredity that gave things he had never seen before a seeming familiarity; the instincts (which were but the memories of his ancestors become habits) which had lapsed in later days, and still later, in him, quickened and become alive again.

Sometimes as he crouched there, blinking dreamily at the flames, it seemed that the flames were of another fire, and that as he crouched by this other fire he saw another and different man from the half-breed cook before him. This other man was shorter of leg and longer of arm, with muscles that were stringy and knotty rather than rounded and swelling. The hair of this man was long and matted, and his head slanted back under it from the eyes. He uttered strange sounds, and seemed very much afraid of the darkness, into which he peered continually, clutching in his hand, which hung midway between knee and foot, a stick with a heavy stone made fast to the end. He was all but naked, a ragged and fire-scorched skin hanging part way down his back, but on his body there was much hair. In some places, across the chest and shoulders and down the outside of the arms and thighs, it was matted into almost a thick fur. He did not stand erect, but with trunk inclined forward from the hips, on legs that bent at the knees. About his body there was a peculiar springiness, or resiliency, almost catlike, and a quick alertness as of one who lived in perpetual fear of things seen and unseen.

At other times this hairy man squatted by the fire with head between his legs and slept. On such occasions his elbows were on his knees, his hands clasped above his head as though to

shed rain by the hairy arms. And beyond that fire, in the circling darkness, Buck could see many gleaming coals, two by two, always two by two, which he knew to be the eyes of great beasts of prey. And he could hear the crashing of their bodies through the undergrowth, and the noise they made in the night. And dreaming there by the Yukon bank, with lazy eyes blinking at the fire, these sounds and sights of another world would make the hair to rise along his back and stand on end across his shoulders and up his neck, till he whimpered low and suppressedly, or growled softly, and the half-breed cook shouted at him, "Hey, you Buck, wake up!" Whereupon the other world would vanish and the real world come into his eyes, and he would get up and yawn and stretch as though he had been asleep.

It was a hard trip, with the mail behind them, and the heavy work wore them down. They were short of weight and in poor condition when they made Dawson, and should have had a ten days' or a week's rest at least. But in two days' time they dropped down the Yukon bank from the Barracks, loaded with letters for the outside. The dogs were tired, the drivers grumbling, and, to make matters worse, it snowed every day. This meant a soft trail, greater friction on the runners, and heavier pulling for the dogs; yet the drivers were fair through it all, and did their best for the animals.

Sleds carried the miner's necessities along with some optional items: a washing-pan (a bowl used to sift through river gravel to extract gold), sieves, shovels, pickaxes, a stove, indispensable for hot meals; crucial food supplies such as sacks of beans, salted beef, and fruit preserves to fight off scurvy, an illness that comes with under-nourishment and lack of vitamin C; and such personal items as books, the Bible, their harmonicas or fiddles, and of course, guns.

Each night the dogs were attended to first. They ate before the drivers ate, and no man sought his sleeping-robe till he had seen to the feet of the dogs he drove. Still, their strength went down. Since the beginning of the winter they had traveled eighteen hundred miles, dragging sleds the whole weary distance; and eighteen hundred miles will tell upon life of the toughest. Buck stood it, keeping his mates up to their work and maintaining discipline, though he, too, was very tired. Billee cried and whimpered regularly in his sleep each night. Joe was sourer than ever, and Sol-leks was unapproachable, blind side or other side.

But it was Dave who suffered most of all. Something had gone wrong with him. He became more morose and irritable, and when camp was pitched at once made his nest, where his driver fed him. Once out of the harness and down, he did not get on his

The husky is a powerful dog. On the average the male weighs between 80 and 110 pounds (36 and 51 kilos) and the female between 70 and 95 pounds (32 and 43 kilos), but some males can grow to over 130 pounds (60 kilos). Six or eight dogs of this size harnessed to a sled can easily pull two men and their baggage.

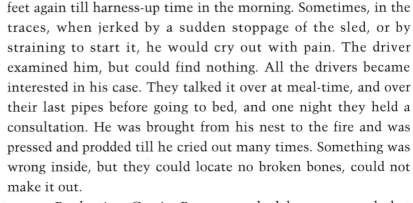

66 Something was wrong inside, but they could locate no broken bones. 99

feet again till harness-up time in the morning. Sometimes, in the traces, when jerked by a sudden stoppage of the sled, or by straining to start it, he would cry out with pain. The driver examined him, but could find nothing. All the drivers became interested in his case. They talked it over at meal-time, and over their last pipes before going to bed, and one night they held a consultation. He was brought from his nest to the fire and was pressed and prodded till he cried out many times. Something was wrong inside, but they could locate no broken bones, could not make it out.

By the time Cassiar Bar was reached, he was so weak that he was falling repeatedly in the traces. The Scotch half-breed called a halt and took him out of the team, making the next dog, Sol-leks, fast to the sled. His intention was to rest Dave, letting him run free behind the sled. Sick as he was, Dave resented being taken out, grunting and growling while the traces were unfastened, and whimpering broken-heartedly when he saw Sol-leks in the position he had held and served so long. For the pride of trace and trail was his, and sick unto death, he could not bear that another dog should do his work.

When the sled started, he floundered in the soft snow alongside the beaten trail, attacking Sol-leks with his teeth, rushing against him and trying to thrust him off into the soft snow on the other side,

striving to leap inside his traces and get between him and the sled, and all the while whining and yelping and crying with grief and pain. The half-breed tried to drive him away with the whip; but he paid no heed to the stinging lash, and the man had not the heart to strike harder. Dave refused to run quietly on the trail behind the sled, where the going was easy, but continued to flounder alongside in the soft snow, where the going was most difficult, till exhausted. Then he fell, and lay where he fell, howling lugubriously as the long train of sleds churned by.

With the last remnant of his strength he managed to stagger along behind till the train made another stop, when he floundered past the sleds to his own, where he stood alongside Sol-leks. His driver lingered a moment to get a light for his pipe from the man behind. Then he returned and started his dogs. They swung out on the trail with remarkable lack of exertion, turned their heads uneasily, and stopped in surprise. The driver was surprised, too; the sled had not moved. He called his comrades to witness the sight. Dave had bitten through both of Sol-leks's traces, and was standing directly in front of the sled in his proper place.

He pleaded with his eyes to remain there. The driver was perplexed. His comrades talked of how a dog could break its heart through being denied the work that killed it, and recalled instances they had known, where dogs, too old for the toil, or injured, had died because they were cut out of the traces. Also, they held it a mercy, since Dave was to die anyway, that he should die in the traces, heart-easy and content. So he was harnessed in again, and proudly he pulled as of old, though more than once he cried out involuntarily from the bite of his inward

A funeral party in winter at Dawson City with the coffin mounted on a sled. The hardness of the frozen soil rarely permitted burial under even a thin layer of earth. Deaths were frequent among the prospectors: the men were exhausted, poorly fed, and scurvy-ridden. Brawls, common in bars, also claimed victims.

hurt. Several times he fell down and was dragged in the traces, and once the sled ran upon him so that he limped thereafter in one of his hind legs.

But he held out till camp was reached, when his driver made a place for him by the fire. Morning found him too weak to travel. At harness-up time he tried to crawl to his driver. By convulsive efforts he got on his feet, staggered, and fell. Then he wormed his way forward slowly toward where the harnesses were being put on his mates. He would advance his forelegs and drag up his body with a sort of hitching movement, when he would advance his forelegs and hitch ahead again for a few more inches. His strength left him, and the last his mates saw of him he lay gasping in the snow and yearning toward them. But they could hear him mournfully howling, till they passed out of sight behind a belt of river timber.

> 66 His strength left him, and the last his mates saw of him he lay gasping in the snow. 99

Here the train was halted. The Scotch half-breed slowly retraced his steps to the camp they had left. The men ceased talking. A revolver-shot rang out. The man came back hurriedly. The whips snapped, the bells tinkled merrily, the sleds churned along the trail; but Buck knew, and every dog knew, what had taken place behind the belt of river trees.

5

THE TOIL OF TRACE AND TRAIL

Thirty days from the time it left Dawson, the Salt Water Mail, with Buck and his mates at the fore, arrived at Skagway. They were in a wretched state, worn out and worn down. Buck's one hundred and forty pounds had dwindled to one hundred and fifteen. The rest of his mates, though lighter dogs, had relatively lost more weight than he. Pike, the malingerer, who, in his lifetime of deceit, had often successfully feigned a hurt leg, was now limping in earnest. Sol-leks was limping, and Dub was suffering from a wrenched shoulder-blade.

They were all terribly footsore. No spring or rebound was left in them. Their feet fell heavily on the trail, jarring their bodies and doubling the fatigue of a day's travel. There was nothing the matter with them except that they were dead tired. It was not the dead-tiredness that comes through brief and excessive effort, from which recovery is a matter of hours; but it was the dead-tiredness that comes through the slow and prolonged strength drainage of months of toil. There was no power of recuperation left, no reserve strength to call upon. It had been all used, the last least bit of it. Every muscle, every fiber, every cell, was tired, dead tired. And there was reason for it. In less than five months they had traveled twenty-five hundred miles, during the last eighteen hundred of which they had had

When prospecting came to an end in the Klondike, it spread elsewhere. In 1902, prospectors came to the Tanara River in the Yukon, and later to Porcupine Valley. Skagway (*above*) was to experience a new gold rush in 1925, when large steamers pulled into its harbor.

Prospectors at Porcupine Hill on the Skagway Trail, which leads to White Pass. Porcupine Hill was feared because of the numerous blocks of stone that cluttered its path.

but five days' rest. When they arrived at Skagway they were apparently on their last legs. They could barely keep the traces taut, and on the down grades just managed to keep out of the way of the sled.

"Mush on, poor sore feets," the driver encouraged them as they tottered down the main street of Skagway. "Dis is de las'. Den we get one long res'. Eh? For sure. One bully long res'."

The drivers confidently expected a long stopover. Themselves, they had covered twelve hundred miles with two days' rest, and in the nature of reason and common justice they deserved an interval of loafing. But so many were the men who had rushed into the Klondike, and so many were the sweethearts, wives, and kin that had not rushed in, that the congested mail was taking on Alpine proportions; also there were official orders. Fresh batches of Hudson Bay dogs were to take the places of those worthless for the trail. The worthless ones were to be got rid of, and since dogs count for little against dollars, they were to be sold.

66 Two men from the States came along and bought them, harness and all, for a song. **99**

Three days passed, by which time Buck and his mates found how really tired and weak they were. Then, on the morning of the fourth day, two men from the States came along and bought them, harness and all, for a song. The men addressed each other as "Hal" and "Charles." Charles was a middle-aged, lightish-colored man, with weak and watery eyes and a moustache that twisted fiercely and vigorously up, giving the lie to the limply drooping lip it concealed. Hal was a youngster of nineteen or twenty, with a big Colt's revolver and a hunting-knife strapped about him on a belt that fairly bristled with cartridges. This belt was the most salient thing about him. It advertised his callowness—a callowness sheer and unutterable. Both men were manifestly out of place, and why such as they should adventure the North is part of the mystery of things that passes understanding.

Buck heard the chaffering, saw the money pass between the man and the Government agent, and knew that the Scotch

half-breed and the mail-train drivers were passing out of his life on the heels of Perrault and François and the others who had gone before. When driven with his mates to the new owners' camp, Buck saw a slipshod and slovenly affair, tent half stretched, dishes unwashed, everything in disorder; also, he saw a woman. "Mercedes" the men called her. She was Charles's wife and Hal's sister—a nice family party.

Buck watched them apprehensively as they proceeded to take down the tent and load the sled. There was a great deal of effort about their manner, but no business-like method. The tent was rolled into an awkward bundle three times as large as it should have been. The tin dishes were packed away unwashed. Mercedes continually fluttered in the way of her men and kept up an unbroken chattering of remonstrance

and advice. When they put a clothes-sack on the front of the sled, she suggested it should go on the back; and when they had put it on the back, and covered it over with a couple of other bundles, she discovered overlooked articles which could abide nowhere else but in that sack, and they unloaded again.

Three men from a neighboring tent came out and looked on, grinning and winking at one another.

"You've got a right smart load as it is," said one of them; "and it's not me should tell you your business, but I wouldn't

This prospector, shown cooking on his overturned sled, is wearing Indian-made clothes of warm, weatherproof caribou hide; the fringe is a conduit for rainwater.

tote that tent along if I was you."

"Undreamed of!" cried Mercedes, throwing up her hands in dainty dismay. "However in the world could I manage without a tent?"

"It's springtime, and you won't get any more cold weather," the man replied.

She shook her head decidedly, and Charles and Hal put the last odds and ends on top the mountainous load.

"Think it'll ride?" one of the men asked.

"Why shouldn't it?" Charles demanded rather shortly.

"Oh, that's all right, that's all right," the man hastened meekly to say. "I was just a-wonderin', that is all. It seemed a mite top-heavy."

Charles turned his back and drew the lashing down as well as he could, which was not in the least well.

"An' of course the dogs can hike along all day with that contraption behind them," affirmed a second of the men.

"Certainly," said Hal, with freezing politeness, taking hold of the gee-pole with one hand and swinging his whip from the other. "Mush!" he shouted. "Mush on there!"

The dogs sprang against the breast-bands, strained hard for a few moments, then relaxed. They were unable to move the sled.

"The lazy brutes, I'll show them," he cried, preparing to

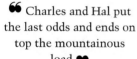

❝ Charles and Hal put the last odds and ends on top the mountainous load. ❞

lash out at them with the whip.

But Mercedes interfered, crying, "Oh, Hal, you mustn't," as she caught hold of the whip and wrenched it from him. "The poor dears! Now you must promise you won't be harsh with them for the rest of the trip, or I won't go a step."

"Precious lot you know about dogs," her brother sneered; "and I wish you'd leave me alone. They're lazy, I tell you, and you've got to whip them to get anything out of them. That's their way. You ask anyone. Ask one of those men."

Mercedes looked at them imploringly, untold repugnance at sight of pain written in her pretty face.

"They're weak as water, if you want to know," came the reply from one of the men. "Plum tuckered out, that's what's the matter. They need a rest."

"Rest be blanked," said Hal, with his beardless lips; and Mercedes said, "Oh!" in pain and sorrow at the oath.

But she was a clannish creature, and rushed at once to the defense of her brother. "Never mind that man," she said pointedly. "You're driving our dogs, and you do what you think best with them."

Again Hal's whip fell upon the dogs. They threw themselves against the breast-bands, dug their feet into the packed snow, got down low to it, and put forth all their strength. The sled held as though it were an anchor. After two efforts, they stood still, panting. The whip was whistling savagely, when once more Mercedes interfered. She dropped on her knees before Buck, with tears in her eyes, and put her arms around his neck.

"You poor, poor dears," she cried sympathetically, "why don't you pull hard?—then you wouldn't be whipped." Buck did not like her, but he was feeling too miserable to resist her, taking it as part of the day's miserable work.

One of the onlookers, who had been clenching his teeth

> **❝** 'I'll show them,' he cried, preparing to lash out at them with the whip. **❞**

In rare moments of relaxation on the trail, the prospectors organized and bet on sled races, or had fun sledding downhill in the snow.

In good weather, the prospectors slept in a tent rigged with mosquito netting. They used the mild season for hunting game. *Above*, two men show their arsenal: a Winchester rifle and a holster gun—used not only for hunting but for protection from other men.

to suppress hot speech, now spoke up:

"It's not that I care a whoop what becomes of you, but for the dogs' sakes I just want to tell you, you can help them a mighty lot by breaking out that sled. The runners are froze fast. Throw your weight against the gee-pole, right and left, and break it out."

A third time the attempt was made, but this time, following the advice, Hal broke out the runners which had been frozen to the snow. The overloaded and unwieldy sled forged ahead. Buck and his mates struggled frantically under the rain of blows. A hundred yards ahead the path turned and sloped steeply into the main street. It would have required an experienced man

to keep the top-heavy sled upright, and Hal was not such a man. As they swung on the turn the sled went over, spilling half its load through the loose lashings. The dogs never stopped. The lightened sled bounded on its side behind them. They were angry because of the ill treatment they had received and the unjust load. Buck was raging. He broke into a run, the team following his lead. Hal cried "Whoa! whoa!" but they gave no heed. He tripped and was pulled off his feet. The capsized sled ground over him, and the dogs dashed on up the street, adding to the gaiety of Skagway as they scattered the remainder of the outfit along its chief thoroughfare.

Kind-hearted citizens caught the dogs and gathered up the scattered belongings. Also, they gave advice. Half the load and twice the dogs, if they ever expected to reach Dawson, was what was said. Hal and his sister and brother-in-law listened unwillingly, pitched tent, and overhauled

Inspired by trappers' log cabins, the prospectors' houses were quite humble: one room, two at the most, crammed with men. In the center stood the indispensable stove, used for heating and cooking. Housefront openings were limited to a door and one or two small windows.

CLANCY'S SALOON

66 The dogs never stopped. The lightened sled bounded on its side behind them. **99**

Animal and sled tracks mingle on the frozen expanse of a land that offered most prospectors little but cold and hunger.

the outfit. Canned goods were turned out that made men laugh, for canned goods on the Long Trail is a thing to dream about. "Blankets for a hotel," quoth one of the men who laughed and helped. "Half as many is too much; get rid of them. Throw away the tent, and all those dishes—who's going to wash them, anyway? Good Lord, do you think you're traveling on a Pullman?"

And so it went, the inexorable elimination of the superfluous. Mercedes cried when her clothes-bags were dumped on the ground and article after article was thrown out. She cried in general, and she cried in particular over each discarded thing. She clasped hands about knees, rocking back and forth broken-heartedly. She averred she would not go an inch, not for a dozen Charleses. She appealed to everybody and to everything, finally wiping her eyes and proceeding to cast out even articles of apparel that were imperative necessities. And in her zeal, when she had finished with her own, she attacked the belongings of her men and went through them like a tornado.

This accomplished, the outfit, though cut in half, was still a formidable bulk. Charles and Hal went out in the evening and bought in six Outside dogs. These, added to the six of the original team, and Teek and Koona, the huskies obtained at the Rink Rapids on the record trip, brought the team up to fourteen. But the Outside dogs, though practically broken in since their landing, did not

amount to much. Three were short-haired pointers, one was a New-foundland, and the other two were mongrels of indeterminate breed. They did not seem to know anything, these newcomers. Buck and his comrades looked upon them with disgust, and

though he speedily taught them their places and what not to do, he could not teach them what to do. They did not take kindly to trace and trail. With the exception of the two mongrels, they were bewildered and spirit-broken by the strange savage environment in which they found themselves and by the ill-treatment they had received. The two mongrels were without spirit at all; bones were the only things breakable about them.

These prospectors are using angora goats as draught animals to pull a supply sled. The little house rising among the tents is for food storage. It is elevated in order to remain stable after the thaw; its sloping roof retains a layer of snow in winter, making for excellent insulation against the cold.

With the newcomers hopeless and forlorn, and the old team worn out by twenty-five hundred miles of continuous trail, the outlook was anything but bright. The two men, however, were quite cheerful. And they were proud, too. They were doing the thing in style, with fourteen dogs. They had seen other sleds depart over the Pass for Dawson, or come in from Dawson, but never had they seen a sled with so many as fourteen dogs. In the nature of Arctic travel there was a reason why fourteen dogs should not drag one sled, and that was that one sled could not carry the food for fourteen dogs. But Charles and Hal did not know this. They worked the trip out with a pencil, so much to a dog, so many dogs, so many days, Q.E.D. Mercedes looked over their shoulders and nodded comprehensively, it was all so very simple.

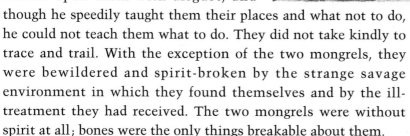

Late next morning Buck led the long team up the street. There was nothing lively about it, no snap or go in him and his fellows. They were starting dead weary. Four times he had covered the distance between Salt Water and Dawson, and the knowledge that, jaded and tired, he was facing the same trail once more, made him bitter. His heart was not in the work, nor was the heart

66 Late next morning Buck led the long team up the street. 99

of any dog. The Outsides were timid and frightened, the Insides without confidence in their masters.

Buck felt vaguely that there was no depending upon these two men and woman. They did not know how to do anything, and as the days went by it became apparent that they could not learn. They were slack in all things, without order or discipline. It took them half the night to pitch a slovenly camp, and half the morning to break that camp and get the sled loaded in fashion so slovenly that for the rest of the day they were occupied in stopping and rearranging the load. Some days they did not make ten miles. On other days they were unable to get started at all. And on no day did they succeeded in making more than half the distance used by the men as a basis in their dog-food computation.

It was inevitable that they should go short on dog-food. But they hastened it by over-feeding, bringing the day nearer when under-feeding would commence. The Outside dogs, whose digestions had not been trained by chronic famine to make the most of little, had voracious appetites. And when, in addition to this, the worn-out huskies pulled weakly, Hal decided that the orthodox ration was too small. He doubled it. And to cap it all, when Mercedes, with tears in her pretty eyes and a quaver in her throat, could not cajole him into giving the dogs still more, she stole from the fish-sacks and fed them slyly. But it was not food that Buck and the huskies needed, but rest. And though they were making poor time, the heavy load they dragged sapped their strength severely.

Then came the under-feeding. Hal awoke one day to the fact that his dog-food was half gone and the distance only quarter

At twenty, Jack London discovered the Klondike and dogs. He developed a passion for huskies and wolves, whose howls he heard during his brief stay in the Northwest.

covered; further, that for love or money no additional dog-food was to be obtained. So he cut down even the orthodox ration and tried to increase the day's travel. His sister and brother-in-law seconded him; but they were frustrated by their heavy outfit and their own incompetence. It was a simple matter to give the dogs less food; but it was impossible to make the dogs travel faster, while their own inability to get under way earlier in the morning prevented them from travelling longer hours. Not only did they not know how to work the dogs, but they did not know how to work themselves.

The first to go was Dub. Poor blundering thief that he was, always getting caught and punished, he had none the less been a faithful worker. His wrenched shoulder-blade, untreated and unrested, went from bad to worse, till finally Hal shot him with the big Colt's revolver. It is a saying of the country that an Outside dog starves to death on the ration of the husky, so the six Outside dogs under Buck could do no less than die on half the ration of the husky. The Newfoundland went first, followed by the three short-haired pointers, the two mongrels hanging more grittily on to life, but going in the end.

By this time all the amenities and gentleness of the Southland had fallen away from the three people. Shorn of its glamour and romance, Arctic travel became to them a reality too harsh for their manhood and womanhood. Mercedes ceased weeping over the dogs, being too occupied with weeping over herself and with quarreling with her husband and brother. To quarrel was the one thing they were never too weary to do. Their irritability arose out of their misery, increased with it, doubled upon it, outdistanced it. The wonderful patience of the trail

After his novel *The Call of the Wild*, London gave up the theme of sled dogs and in *White Fang*, tells the story of a wolf and its friendship with a young man.

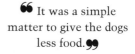

66 It was a simple matter to give the dogs less food. **99**

In winter the prospectors made their way over frozen lakes, the forest trails being often too snowy. However, a warm wind, sun, the least rise of temperature could weaken the ice surface and cause it to break, especially when the sleds were carrying heavy loads. And woe to the man too impatient to light a large fire for drying his clothes; he risked dying of cold when they froze on him!

66 A toothless old squaw offered to trade them a few pounds of frozen horse-hide for the Colt's revolver.99

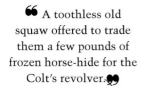

which comes to men who toil hard and suffer sore, and remain sweet of speech and kindly, did not come to these two men and the woman. They had no inkling of such a patience. They were stiff and in pain; their muscles ached, their bones ached, their very hearts ached; and because of this they became sharp of speech, and hard words were first on their lips in the morning and last at night.

Charles and Hal wrangled whenever Mercedes gave them a chance. It was the cherished belief of each that he did more than his share of the work, and neither forbore to speak this belief at every opportunity. Sometimes Mercedes sided with her husband, sometimes with her brother. The result was a beautiful and unending family quarrel. Starting from a dispute as to which should chop a few sticks for the fire (a dispute which concerned only Charles and Hal), presently would be lugged in the rest of the family, fathers, mothers, uncles, cousins, people thousands of miles away and some of them dead. That Hal's views on art, or the sort of society plays his mother's brother wrote, should have anything to do with the chopping of a few sticks of firewood, passes comprehension; nevertheless the quarrel was as likely to tend in that direction as in the direction of Charles's political prejudices. And that Charles's sister's tale-bearing tongue should be relevant to the building of a Yukon fire, was apparent only to Mercedes, who disburdened herself of copious opinions upon that topic, and incidentally upon a few other traits unpleasantly peculiar to her husband's family. In the meantime the fire remained unbuilt, the camp half pitched, and the dogs unfed.

Mercedes nursed a special grievance—the grievance of her sex. She was pretty and soft, and had been chivalrously treated all her days. But the present treatment by her husband and brother was everything save chivalrous.

It was her custom to be helpless. They complained. Upon which impeachment of what to her was her most essential sex-prerogative, she made their lives unendurable. She no longer considered the dogs, and because she was sore and tired, she persisted in riding on the sled. She was pretty and soft, but she weighed one hundred and twenty pounds—a lusty last straw to the load dragged by the weak and starving animals. She rode for days, till they fell in the traces and the sled stood still. Charles and Hal begged her to get off and walk, pleaded with her, entreated, the while she wept and importuned Heaven with a recital of their brutality. On one occasion they took her off the sled by main strength. They never did it again. She let her legs go limp like a spoiled child, and sat down on the trail. They went on their way, but she did not move. After they had traveled three miles they unloaded the sled, came back for her, and by main strength put her on the sled again.

In the excess of their own misery they were callous to the suffering of their animals. Hal's theory, which he practised on others, was that one must get hardened. He had started out preaching it to his sister and brother-in-law. Failing there, he hammered it into the dogs with a club. At the Five Fingers the dog-food gave out, and a toothless old squaw offered to trade them a few pounds of frozen horse-hide for the Colt's revolver that kept the big hunting-knife company at Hal's hip. A poor substitute for food was this hide, just as it had been stripped from the starved horses of the cattlemen six months back. In its frozen state it was more like strips of galvanized iron, and when a dog wrestled it into his stomach it thawed into thin and innutritious leathery strings and into a mass of short hair, irritating and indigestible.

And through it all Buck staggered along at the head of the team as in a nightmare. He pulled when he could; when he could no longer pull, he fell down and remained till blows from whip or club drove him to his feet again. All the stiffness and gloss had gone out of his beautiful furry coat. The hair hung down, limp and

66 Hal had traded off his revolver so he took the axe and knocked Billee on the head. 99

❝ The ghostly winter silence had given way to the great spring murmur of awakening life. **❞**

In spring, the Northern forest (*above*) regains its colors: ponds, swamps, and lakes are dotted with a live covering of aspens, maples, birches, and pines. The Canadian grouse (*below*) is a favorite game bird.

draggled, or matted with dried blood where Hal's club had bruised him. His muscles had wasted away to knotty strings, and the flesh pads had disappeared, so that each rib and every bone in his frame were outlined cleanly through the loose hide that was wrinkled in folds of emptiness. It was heartbreaking, only Buck's heart was unbreakable. The man in the red sweater had proved that.

As it was with Buck, so it was with his mates. They were perambulating skeletons. There were seven all together, including him. In their very great misery they had become insensible to the bite of the lash or the bruise of the club. The pain of the beating was dull and distant, just as the things their eyes saw and their ears heard seemed dull and distant. They were not half living, or quarter living. They were simply so many bags of bones in which sparks of life fluttered faintly. When a halt was made, they dropped down in the traces like dead dogs, and the spark dimmed and paled and seemed to go out. And when the club or whip fell upon them, the spark fluttered feebly up, and they tottered to their feet and staggered on.

There came a day when Billee, the good-natured, fell and could not rise. Hal had traded off his revolver, so he took the axe and knocked Billee on the head as he lay in the traces, then cut the carcass out of the harness and dragged it to one side. Buck saw, and his mates saw, and they knew that this thing was very close to them. On the next day Koona went, and but five of them remained: Joe, too far gone to be malignant; Pike, crippled and limping, only half conscious and not conscious enough longer to malinger; Sol-leks, the one-eyed, still faithful to the toil of trace

and trail, and mournful in that he had so little strength with which to pull; Teek, who had not traveled so far that winter and who was now beaten more than the others because he was fresher; and Buck, still at the head of the team, but no longer enforcing discipline or striving to enforce it, blind with weakness half the time and keeping the trail by the loom of it and by the dim feel of his feet.

It was beautiful spring weather, but neither dogs nor humans were aware of it. Each day the sun rose earlier and set later. It was dawn by three in the morning, and twilight lingered till nine at night. The whole long day was a blaze of sunshine. The ghostly winter silence had given way to the great spring murmur of awakening life. The murmur arose from all the land, fraught with the joy of living. It came from the things that lived and moved again, things which had been as dead and which had not moved during the long months of frost. The sap was rising in the pines. The willows and aspens were bursting out in young buds. Shrubs and vines were putting on fresh garbs of green. Crickets sang in the nights, and in the days all manner of creeping, crawling things rustled forth into the sun. Partridges and woodpeckers were booming and knocking in the forest. Squirrels were chattering, birds singing, and overhead honked the wild-fowl driving up from the south in cunning wedges that split the air.

From every hill slope came the trickle of running water, the music of unseen fountains. All things were thawing, bending, snapping. The Yukon was straining to break loose the ice that bound it down. It ate away from beneath; the sun ate from above. Air-holes formed, fissures sprang and spread apart, while thin sections of ice fell through bodily into the river. And amid all this bursting, rending, throbbing of awakening life, under the blazing sun and through the soft-sighing breezes, like wayfarers to death, staggered the two men, the woman, and the huskies.

66 John Thornton was whittling the last touches of an axe-handle he had made from a stick of birch. 99

The bald eagle circles the lakes, swooping down when fish surface.

Two essential items for the prospector were a hat and boots, to protect head and feet from the cold. Their feet got quite a workout, between the spongy soil of the northern forest in summer, and the muddy trails in spring.

66 'Only fools could have made it.'99

With the dogs falling, Mercedes weeping and riding, Hal swearing innocuously, and Charles's eyes wistfully watering, they staggered into John Thornton's camp at the mouth of White River. When they halted, the dogs dropped down as though they had all been struck dead. Mercedes dried her eyes and looked at John Thornton. Charles sat down on a log to rest. He sat down very slowly and painstakingly because of his great stiffness. Hal did the talking. John Thornton was whittling the last touches of an axe-handle he had made from a stick of birch. He whittled and listened, gave monosyllabic replies, and, when it was asked, terse advice. He knew the breed, and he gave his advice in the certainty that it would not be followed.

"They told us up above that the bottom was dropping out of the trail and that the best thing for us to do was to lay over," Hal said in response to Thornton's warning to take no more chances on the rotten ice. "They told us we couldn't make White River, and here we are." This last with a sneering ring of triumph in it.

"And they told you true," John Thornton answered. "The bottom's likely to drop out at any moment. Only fools, with the blind luck of fools, could have made it. I tell you straight, I wouldn't risk my carcass on that ice for all the gold in Alaska."

"That's because you're not a fool, I suppose," said Hal. "All the same, we'll go on to Dawson." He uncoiled his whip. "Get up there, Buck! Hi! Get up there! Mush on!"

Thornton went on whittling. It was idle, he knew, to get between a fool and his folly; while two or three fools more or less would not alter the scheme of things.

But the team did not get up at the command. It had long since passed into the stage where blows were required to rouse it. The whip flashed out, here and there, on its merciless errands. John Thornton compressed his lips. Sol-leks was the first to crawl to his feet. Teek followed. Joe came next, yelping with pain. Pike made painful efforts. Twice he fell over, when half up, and on the third attempt managed to rise. Buck made no effort. He lay quietly where he had fallen. The lash bit into him again and again, but he neither whined nor struggled. Several times Thornton started, as though to speak, but changed his mind. A

moisture came into his eyes, and, as the whipping continued, he arose and walked irresolutely up and down.

This was the first time Buck had failed, in itself a sufficient reason to drive Hal into a rage. He exchanged the whip for the customary club. Buck refused to move under the rain of heavier blows which now fell upon him. Like his mates, he was barely able to get up, but, unlike them, he had made up his mind not to get up. He had a vague feeling of impending doom. This had been strong upon him when he pulled in to the bank, and it had not departed from him. What of the thin and rotten ice he had felt under his feet all day, it seemed that he sensed disaster close at hand, out there ahead on the ice where his master was trying to drive him. He refused to stir. So greatly had he suffered, and so far gone was he, that the blows did not hurt much. And as they continued to fall upon him, the spark of life within flickered and went down. It was nearly out. He felt strangely numb. As though from a great distance, he was aware that he was being beaten. The last sensations of pain left him. He no longer felt anything, though very faintly he could hear the impact of the club upon his body. But it was no longer his body, it seemed so far away.

Every prospector carried his personal effects on his back: a change of clothes, a stock of food—most of it preserved—and always one or two good woolen blankets rolled up on top of the sack.

And then, suddenly, without warning, uttering a cry that was inarticulate and more like the cry of an animal, John Thornton sprang upon the man who wielded the club. Hal was hurled backward, as though struck by a falling tree. Mercedes screamed. Charles looked on wistfully, wiping his watery eyes, but did not get up because of his stiffness.

John Thornton stood over Buck, struggling to control himself, too convulsed with rage to speak.

"If you strike that dog again, I'll kill you," he at last managed to say in a choking voice.

"It's my dog," Hal replied, wiping the blood from his mouth as he came back. "Get out of my way, or I'll fix you. I'm going to Dawson."

Thornton stood between him and Buck, and evinced no intention of getting out of the way. Hal drew his long hunting-knife. Mercedes screamed, cried, laughed and manifested the chaotic abandonment of hysteria. Thornton rapped Hal's knuckles with the axe-handle, knocking the knife to the ground. He rapped his knuckles again as he tried to pick it up. Then he stooped,

66 A yawning hole was all that was to be seen. 99

picked it up himself, and with two strokes cut Buck's traces.

Hal had no fight left in him. Besides, his hands were full with his sister, or his arms, rather; while Buck was too near dead to be of further use in hauling the sled. A few minutes later they pulled out from the bank and down the river. Buck heard them go and raised his head to see. Pike was leading, Sol-leks was at the wheel, and between were Joe and Teek. They were limping and staggering. Mercedes was riding the loaded sled. Hal guided at the gee-pole, and Charles stumbled along in the rear.

As Buck watched them, Thornton knelt beside him and with rough, kindly hands searched for broken bones. By the time his search had disclosed nothing more than many bruises and a state of terrible starvation, the sled was a quarter of a mile away. Dog and man watched it crawling along over the ice. Suddenly, they saw its back end drop down, as into a rut, and the gee-pole, with Hal clinging to it, jerk into the air. Mercedes's scream came

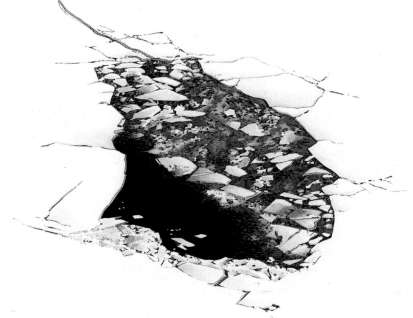

to their ears. They saw Charles turn and make one step to run back, and then a whole section of ice gave way and dogs and humans disappeared. A yawning hole was all that was to be seen. The bottom had dropped out of the trail.

John Thornton and Buck looked at each other.

"You poor devil," said John Thornton, and Buck licked his hand.

6

FOR THE LOVE OF A MAN

When John Thornton froze his feet in the previous December, his partners had made him comfortable and left him to get well, going on themselves up the river to get out a raft of saw-logs for Dawson. He was still limping slightly at the time he rescued Buck, but with the continued warm weather even the slight limp left him. And here, lying by the river bank through the long spring days, watching the running water, listening lazily to the songs of birds and the hum of nature, Buck slowly won back his strength.

A rest comes very good after one has traveled three thousand miles, and it must be confessed that Buck waxed lazy as his wounds healed, his muscles swelled out, and the flesh came back to cover his bones. For that matter, they were all

66 Here, listening lazily to the songs of birds and the hum of nature, Buck slowly won back his strength. **99**

85

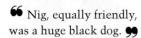

66 Skeet was a little Irish setter. 99

66 Nig, equally friendly, was a huge black dog. 99

The Northern forest has no underbrush. Its soil is covered in a thick, spongy brown-ish carpet formed by accumulated pine and spruce needles. On the shores of rivers and lakes grow broad-leaved trees, among them the silver birch, prized for its use as paper pulp.

loafing—Buck, John Thornton, and Skeet and Nig—waiting for the raft to come that was to carry them down to Dawson. Skeet was a little Irish setter who early made friends with Buck, who, in a dying condition, was unable to resent her first advances. She had the doctor trait which some dogs possess; and as a mother cat washes her kittens, so she washed and cleansed Buck's wounds. Regularly, each morning, after he had finished his breakfast, she performed her self-appointed task, till he came to look for her ministrations as much as he did for Thornton's. Nig, equally friendly, though less demonstrative, was a huge black dog, half bloodhound and half deerhound, with eyes that laughed and a boundless good nature.

To Buck's surprise these dogs manifested no jealousy toward him. They seemed to share the kindliness and largeness of John Thornton. As Buck grew stronger they enticed him into all sorts of ridiculous games, in which Thornton himself could not forbear to join; and in this fashion Buck romped through his convalescence and into a new existence. Love, genuine passionate love, was his for the first time. This he had never experienced at Judge Miller's down in the sun-kissed Santa Clara Valley. With the Judge's son, hunting and tramping, it had been a working partnership; with the Judge's grandsons, a sort of pompous guardianship; and with the Judge himself, a stately and dignified friendship. But love that was feverish and burning, that was adoration, that was madness, it had taken John Thornton to arouse.

This man had saved his life, which was something; but, further, he was the ideal master. Other men saw to the welfare of their dogs from a sense of duty and business expediency; he saw to the welfare of his as if they were his own children, because he could not help it. And he saw further. He never forgot a kindly greeting or a cheering word, and to sit down for a long talk with them ("gas" he called it) was as much his delight as theirs. He had a way of taking Buck's head roughly between his hands, and resting his own head upon Buck's, of shaking him back and forth, the while calling him ill names that to Buck were love names. Buck knew no greater joy than that rough embrace and the sound of murmured oaths, and at each jerk back and forth it seemed

that his heart would be shaken out of his body so great was its ecstasy. And when, released, he sprang to his feet, his mouth laughing, his eyes eloquent, his throat vibrant with unuttered sounds, and in that fashion remained without movement, John Thornton would reverently exclaim, "God, you can all but speak!"

Buck had a trick of love expression that was akin to hurt. He would often seize Thornton's hand in his mouth and close so fiercely that the flesh bore impress of his teeth for some time afterwards. And as Buck understood the oaths to be love words, so the man understood this feigned bite for a caress.

For the most part, however, Buck's love was expressed in adoration. While he went wild with happiness when Thornton touched him or spoke to him, he did not seek these tokens. Unlike Skeet, who was wont to shove her nose under Thornton's hand and nudge and nudge till petted, or Nig, who would stalk up and rest his great head on Thornton's knee, Buck was content to adore at a distance. He would lie by the hour, eager, alert, at Thornton's feet looking up into his face, dwelling upon it, studying it, following with keenest interest each fleeting expression, every movement or change of feature. Or, as chance might have it, he would lie farther away, to the side or rear, watching the outlines of the man and the occasional movements of his body. And often, such was the communion in which they lived, the strength of Buck's gaze would draw John Thornton's head around, and he would return the gaze, without speech, his heart shining out of his eyes as Buck's heart shone out.

For a long time after his rescue, Buck did not like Thornton to get out of his sight. From the moment he left the tent to when he entered it again, Buck would follow at his heels. His transient masters since he had come into the Northland had bred in him a fear that no master could be permanent. He was afraid that Thornton would pass out of his life as Perrault and

❝ He was the ideal master. **❞**

Huskies and other dogs often join a pack of wolves and turn wild again. Out of their unions mongrels are born, ancestors of our tamed wolf-dog. Here, a group of strange-headed wolf-dogs share a bull's skull.

66 He was a thing of the wild, come in from the wild to sit by John Thornton's fire. 99

François and the Scotch half-breed had passed out. Even in the night, in his dreams, he was haunted by this fear. At such times he would shake off sleep and creep through the chill to the flap of the tent, where he would stand and listen to the sound of his master's breathing.

But in spite of this great love he bore John Thornton, which seemed to bespeak the soft civilizing influence, the strain of the primitive, which the Northland had aroused in him, remained alive and active. Faithfulness and devotion, things born of fire and roof, were his, yet he retained his wildness and wiliness. He was a thing of the wild, come in from the wild to sit by John Thornton's fire, rather than a dog of the soft Southland stamped with the marks of generations of civilization. Because of his very great love, he could not steal from this man, but from any man, in any other camp, he did not hesitate an instant; while the cunning with which he stole enabled him to escape detection.

His face and body were scored by the teeth of many dogs, and he fought as fiercely as ever and more shrewdly. Skeet and Nig were too good-natured for quarreling—besides, they belonged to John Thornton; but the strange dog, no matter what the breed or valour, swiftly acknowledged Buck's supremacy or found himself struggling for life with a terrible antagonist. And Buck was merciless. He had learned well the law of club and fang, and he never forwent an advantage or drew back from a foe he had started on the way to Death. He had lessoned from Spitz, and from the chief fighting dogs of the police and mail, and knew there was no middle course. He must master or be mastered; while to show mercy was a weakness. Mercy did not exist in the primordial life. It was misunderstood for fear, and such misunderstandings made for death. Kill or be killed, eat or be eaten, was the law; and this mandate, down out of the depths of Time, he obeyed.

He was older than the days he had seen and the breaths he had drawn. He linked the past with the present, and the eternity behind him throbbed through him in a mighty rhythm to which he swayed as the tides and seasons swayed. He sat by John Thornton's fire, a broad-breasted dog, white-fanged and

long-furred; but behind him were the shades of all manner of dogs, half-wolves and wild wolves, urgent and prompting, tasting the savour of the meat he ate, thirsting for the water he drank, scenting the wind with him, listening with him and telling him the sounds made by the wild life in the forest, dictating his moods, directing his actions, lying down to sleep with him when he lay down, and dreaming with him and beyond him and becoming themselves the stuff of his dreams.

So peremptorily did these shades beckon him, that each day mankind and the claims of mankind slipped farther from him. Deep in the forest a call was sounding, and as often as he heard this call, mysteriously thrilling and luring, he felt compelled to turn his back upon the fire and the beaten earth around it, and to plunge into the forest, and on and on, he knew not where or why; nor did he wonder where or why, the call sounding imperiously, deep in the forest. But as often as he gained the soft unbroken earth and the green shade, the love for John Thornton drew him back to the fire again.

Thornton alone held him. The rest of mankind was as nothing. Chance travelers might praise or pet him; but he was cold under it all, and from a too demonstrative man he would get up and walk away. When Thornton's partners, Hans and Pete, arrived on the long-expected raft Buck refused to notice them till he learned they were close to Thornton; after that he tolerated them in a passive sort of way, accepting favors from them as though he favored them by accepting. They were of the same large type as Thornton, living close to the earth, thinking simply and seeing clearly; and ere they swung the raft into the big eddy by the sawmill at Dawson, they understood Buck and his ways, and did not insist upon an intimacy such as obtained with Skeet and Nig.

For Thornton, however, his love seemed to grow and grow. He, alone among men, could put a pack upon Buck's back in the summer traveling. Nothing was too great for

> 66 Thornton's partners, Hans and Pete were of the same large type as Thornton, living close to the earth, thinking simply and seeing clearly. 99

Buck to do, when Thornton commanded. One day (they had grub-staked themselves from the proceeds of the raft and left Dawson for the head-waters of the Tanana) the men and dogs were sitting on the crest of a cliff which fell away, straight down, to naked bed-rock three hundred feet below. John Thornton was sitting near the edge. Buck at his shoulder. A thoughtless whim seized Thornton, and he drew the attention of Hans and Pete to the experiment he had in mind. "Jump, Buck!" he commanded, sweeping his arm out and over the chasm. The next instant he was grappling with Buck on the extreme edge, while Hans and Pete were dragging them back into safety.

"It's uncanny," Pete said, after it was over and they caught their speech.

Thornton shook his head. "No, it is splendid, and it is terrible too. Do you know, it sometimes makes me afraid."

"I'm not hankering to be the man that lays hands on you while he's around," Pete announced conclusively, nodding his head toward Buck.

"By Jingo!" was Hans' contribution. "Not mine self either."

It was at Circle City, ere the year was out, that Pete's apprehensions were realized. "Black" Burton, a man evil-tempered and malicious, had been picking a quarrel with a tenderfoot at the bar, when Thornton stepped good-naturedly between. Buck, as was his custom, was lying in a corner, head on paws, watching his master's every action. Burton struck out, without warning, straight from the shoulder. Thornton was sent spinning, and saved himself from falling only by clutching the rail of the bar.

Those who were looking on heard what was neither bark nor yelp, but a something which is best described as a roar, and they saw Buck's body rise up in the air as he left the floor for Burton's throat. The man saved his life by instinctively throwing out his arm, but was hurled backward to the floor with Buck on top of him. Buck loosed his teeth from the flesh of the arm and drove in again for the throat. This time the man succeeded only in partly blocking, and his throat was torn open. Then the crowd was upon Buck, and he was driven off; but while a surgeon

66 Nothing was too great for Buck to do when Thornton commanded. 99

90

checked the bleeding, he prowled up and down, growling furiously, attempting to rush in, and being forced back by an array of hostile clubs. A "miners' meeting," called on the spot, decided that the dog had sufficient provocation, and Buck was discharged. But his reputation was made, and from that day his name spread through every camp in Alaska.

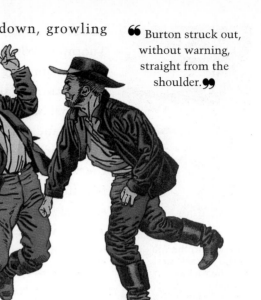

Later on, in the fall of the year, he saved John Thornton's life in quite another fashion. The three partners were lining a long and narrow poling- boat down a bad stretch of rapids on the Forty-Mile Creek. Hans and Pete moved along the bank, snubbing with a thin Manila rope from tree to tree, while Thornton remained in the boat, helping the descent by means of a pole, and shouting directions to the shore. Buck, on the bank, worried and anxious, kept abreast of the boat, his eyes never off his master.

At a particularly bad spot where a ledge of barely submerged rocks jutted out into the river, Hans cast off the rope, and, while Thornton poled the boat out into the stream, ran down the bank with the end in his hand to snub the boat when it had cleared the ledge. This it did, and was flying down-stream in a current as swift as a mill-race, when Hans checked it with the rope and checked too suddenly. The boat flirted over and snubbed into the bank bottom up, while Thornton, flung sheer out of it, was carried down-stream toward the worst part of the rapids, a stretch of wild water in which no swimmer could live.

Buck had sprung in on the instant; and at the end of three

Tensions between men were high. Disappointment and despair at failing to strike it rich, as well as alcohol and gambling, caused violent fights. Boxing matches for betting stakes were also organized in the bars.

91

Strong rafts were built for crossing the major rivers. Prospectors and their Indian porters use a long wooden pole to ford a stream.

66 The boat flirted over and snubbed into the bank bottom up, while Thornton, flung sheer out of it, was carried down-stream toward the worst part of the rapids. 99

hundred yards, amid a mad swirl of water, he overhauled Thornton. When he felt him grasp his tail, Buck headed for the bank, swimming with all his splendid strength. But the progress shoreward was slow; the progress down-stream amazingly rapid. From below came the fatal roaring where the wild current went wilder and was rent in shreds and spray by the rocks which thrust through like the teeth of an enormous comb. The suck of the water as it took the beginning of the last steep pitch was frightful, and Thornton knew that the shore was impossible. He scraped furiously over a rock, bruised across a second, and struck a third with crushing force. He clutched its slippery top with both hands, releasing Buck, and above the roar of the churning water shouted: "Go, Buck! Go!"

Buck could not hold his own, and swept on downstream, struggling desperately, but unable to win back. When he heard Thornton's command repeated, he partly reared out of the water, throwing his head high as through for a last look, then turned obediently toward the bank. He swam powerfully and was dragged ashore by Pete and Hans at the very point where swimming ceased to be possible and destruction began.

They knew that the time a man could cling to a slippery rock in the face of that driving current was a matter of minutes, and they ran as fast as they could up the bank to a point far above

92

where Thornton was hanging on. They attached the line with which they had been snubbing the boat to Buck's neck and shoulders, being careful that it should neither strangle him nor impede his swimming and launched him into the stream. He struck out boldly but not straight enough into the stream. He discovered the mistake too late, when Thornton was abreast of him and a bare half-dozen strokes away while he was being carried helplessly past.

Hans promptly snubbed with the rope, as though Buck were a boat. The rope thus tightening on him in the sweep of the current, he was jerked under the surface, and under the surface he remained till his body struck against the bank and he was hauled out. He was half drowned, and Hans and Pete threw themselves upon him, pounding the breath into him and the water out of him. He staggered to his feet and fell down. The faint sound of Thornton's voice came to them, and though they could not make out the words of it, they knew that he was in his extremity. His master's voice acted on Buck like an electric shock. He sprang to his feet and ran up the bank ahead of the men to the point of his previous departure.

66 He clutched its slippery top with both hands. 99

Again the rope was attached and he was launched, and again he struck out, but this time straight into the stream. He had miscalculated once, but he would not be guilty of it a second time. Hans paid out the rope, permitting no slack, while Pete kept it clear of coils. Buck held on till he was on a line straight above Thornton; then he turned, and with the speed of an express train headed down upon him. Thornton saw him coming, and, as Buck struck him like a battering ram, with the whole force of the current behind him, he reached up and closed with both arms around the shaggy neck. Hans snubbed the rope around the tree, and Buck and

Thornton were jerked under the water. Strangling, suffocating, sometimes one uppermost and sometimes the other, dragging over the jagged bottom, smashing against rocks and snags, they veered in to the bank.

Thornton came to, belly downward and being violently propelled back and forth across a drift log by Hans and Pete. His first glance was for Buck, over whose limp and apparently lifeless body Nig was setting up a howl, while Skeet was licking the wet face and closed eyes. Thornton was himself bruised and battered, and he went carefully over Buck's body, when he had been brought around, finding three broken ribs.

"That settles it," he announced. "We camp right here." And camp they did, till Buck's ribs knitted and he was able to travel.

That winter, at Dawson, Buck performed another exploit, not so heroic, perhaps, but one that put his name many notches higher on the totem-pole of Alaskan fame. This exploit was particularly gratifying to the three men; for they stood in need of the outfit which it furnished, and were enabled to make a long-desired trip into the virgin East, where miners had not yet appeared. It was brought about by a conversation in the Eldorado Saloon, in which men waxed boastful of their favourite dogs. Buck, because of his record, was the target of these men, and Thornton was driven stoutly to defend him. At the end of half an hour one man stated that his dog could start a sled with five hundred pounds and walk off with it; a second bragged six hundred for his dog; and a third, seven hundred.

"Pooh! pooh!" said John Thornton; "Buck can start a thousand pounds."

"And break it out? And walk off with it for a hundred yards?" demanded Matthewson, a Bonanza King, he of the seven hundred vaunt.

"And break it out, and walk off with it for a hundred yards," John Thornton said coolly.

"Well," Matthewson said, slowly and deliberately, so that all could hear, "I've got a thousand dollars that says he can't. And there it

Gang ringleader Soapy Smith terrorized Skagway, where he controlled gambling and prostitution, until his slaying by a rival in July 1898. Skagway, like Dawson City, was a dangerous place; its money lured many con men, prostitutes, and professional gamblers. The Mounted Police were too few to maintain order in a city whose population could triple or quadruple in a matter of weeks.

is." So saying, he slammed a sack of gold dust of the size of a bologna sausage down upon the bar.

Nobody spoke. Thornton's bluff, if bluff it was, had been called. He could feel a flush of warm blood creeping up his face. His tongue had tricked him. He did not know whether Buck could start a thousand pounds. Half a ton! The enormousness of it appalled him. He had great faith in Buck's strength and had often thought him capable of starting such a load; but never, as now, had he faced the possibility of it, the eyes of a dozen men fixed upon him, silent and waiting. Further, he had no thousand dollars; nor had Hans or Pete.

"I've got a sled standing outside now, with twenty fifty-pound sacks of flour on it," Matthewson went on, with brutal directness, "So don't let that hinder you."

Thornton did not reply. He did not know what to say. He glanced from face to face in the absent way of a man who has lost the power of thought and is seeking somewhere to find the thing that will start it going again. The face of Jim O'Brien, a Mastodon King and old-time comrade, caught his eyes. It was a cue to him, seeming to rouse him to do what he would never have dreamed of doing.

66 In the Eldorado Saloon men waxed boastful of their favorite dogs. 99

"Can you lend me a thousand?" he asked, almost in a whisper.

"Sure," answered O'Brien, thumping down a plethoric sack by the side of Matthewson's. "Though it's little faith I'm having, John, that the beast can do the trick."

The easy money of some and the profit-making dreams of others encourage gambling for fantastic sums. For want of horses, bets were placed on dog races. *Above*: a dog team that reached Skagway from Dawson City in under twenty-four hours!

The Eldorado emptied its occupants into the street to see the test. The tables were deserted, and the dealers and gamekeepers came forth to see the outcome of the wager and to lay odds. Several hundred men, furred and mittened, banked around the sled within easy distance. Matthewson's sled, loaded with a thousand pounds of flour, had been standing for a couple of hours, and in the intense cold (it was sixty below zero) the runners had frozen fast to the hard-packed snow. Men offered odds of two to one that Buck could not budge the sled.

A quibble arose concerning the phrase "break out." O'Brien contended it was Thornton's privilege to knock the runners loose, leaving Buck to "break it out" from a dead standstill. Matthewson insisted that the phrase included breaking the runners from the frozen grip of the snow. A majority of the men who had witnessed the making of the bet decided in his favor, whereat the odds went up to three to one against Buck.

There were no takers. Not a man believed him capable of

66 Buck had caught the contagion of the excitement, and he felt that in some way he must do a great thing for John Thornton. 99

the feat. Thornton had been hurried into the wager, heavy with doubt, and now that he looked at the sled itself, the concrete fact, with the regular team of ten dogs curled up on the snow before it, the more impossible the task appeared. Matthewson waxed jubilant.

"Three to one!" he proclaimed. "I'll lay you another thousand at that figure, Thornton. What d'ye say?"

Thornton's doubt was strong in his face, but his fighting spirit was aroused—the fighting spirit that soars above odds, fails to recognize the impossible, and is deaf to all save the clamor for battle. He called Hans and Pete to him. Their sacks were slim, and with his own the three partners could rake together only two hundred dollars. In the ebb of their fortunes, this sum was their total capital; yet they laid it unhesitatingly against Matthewson's six hundred.

Gold nuggets, specks, and dust arrived at the Dawson City banks in little cloth sacks brought by the prospectors; they were weighed and exchanged for money. In 1898, sixty thousand prospectors scoured the whole Klondike region, but very few hit the jackpot. The winners and losers alike inspired Jack London: in *Burning Daylight* he mingles people he actually knew, like Elam Harmish, nicknamed "Burning Daylight," with figures of legend, such as Carmack.

The team of ten dogs was unhitched, and Buck, with his own harness, was put into the sled. He had caught the contagion of the excitement, and he felt that in some way he must do a great thing for John Thornton. Murmurs of admiration at his splendid condition, without an ounce of superfluous flesh, and the one hundred and fifty pounds that he weighed were so many pounds of grit and virility. His furry coat shone with the sheen of silk. Down the neck and across the shoulders, his mane, in respose as it was, half bristled and seemed to lift with every movement, as though excess of vigor made each particular hair alive and active. The great breast and heavy forelegs were no more than in proportion with the rest of the body, where the muscles showed in tight rolls underneath the skin. Men felt these muscles and proclaimed them hard as iron, and the odds went down to two to one.

"Gad, sir! Gad, sir!" stuttered a member of the latest dynasty, a king of the Skookum Benches. "I offer you eight hundred for him, sir, before the test, sir; eight hundred just as he stands."

Thornton shook his head and stepped to Buck's side.

With no police forces, the mining concessions constituted a society based on total trust: cabins were left unlocked, and supplies were shared. Justice was swift, with sentences decided by a show of hands among the men gathered in an improvised tribunal. There were no prison terms; for cases of theft, the punishment was hanging; for lesser crimes, whipping. *Above*: a prospector is hanged for stealing a portion of his neighbor's meal.

"You must stand off from him," Matthewson protested. "Free play and plenty of room."

The crowd fell silent; only could be heard the voices of the gamblers vainly offering two to one. Everybody acknowledged Buck a magnificent animal, but twenty fifty-pound sacks of flour bulked too large in their eyes for them to loosen their pouch-strings.

Thornton knelt down by Buck's side. He took his head in his two hands and rested cheek on cheek. He did not playfully shake him, as was his wont, or murmur soft love curses; but he whispered in his ear. "As you love me, Buck. As you love me," was what he whispered. Buck whined with suppressed eagerness.

The crowd was watching curiously. The affair was growing mysterious. It seemed like a conjuration. As Thornton got to his feet, Buck seized his mittened hand between his jaws, pressing in with his teeth and releasing slowly, half-reluctantly. It was the answer, in terms, not of speech, but of love. Thornton stepped well back.

"Now, Buck," he said.

Buck tightened the traces, then slacked them for a matter of several inches. It was the way he had learned.

"Gee!" Thornton's voice rang out, sharp in the tense silence.

Buck swung to the right, ending the movement in a plunge that took up the slack and with a sudden jerk arrested his one hundred and fifty pounds. The load quivered, and from under the runners arose a crisp crackling.

"Haw!" Thornton commanded.

Buck duplicated the maneuver, this time to the left. The crackling turned into a snapping, the sled pivoting and the runners slipping and grating several inches to the side. The sled was broken out. Men were holding their breaths, intensely unconscious of the fact.

"Now, MUSH!"

Thornton's command cracked out like a pistol-shot. Buck threw himself foward, tightening the traces with a jarring lunge. His whole body was gathered compactly together in the tremendous effort, the muscles writhing and knotting like live

things under the silky fur. His great chest was low to the ground, his head forward and down, while his feet were flying like mad, the claws scarring the hard-packed snow in parallel grooves. The sled swayed and trembled, half-started forward. One of his feet slipped, and one man groaned aloud. Then the sled lurched ahead in what appeared a rapid succession of jerks, though it never really came to a dead stop again . . . half an inch . . an inch . . . two inches . . . The jerks perceptibly diminished; as the sled gained momentum, he caught them up, till it was moving steadily along.

Men gasped and began to breathe again, unaware that for a moment they had ceased to breathe. Thornton was running behind, encouraging Buck with short, cheery words. The distance had been measured off, and as he neared the pile of firewood which marked the end of the hundred yards, a cheer began to grow and grow, which burst into a roar as he passed the firewood

❝ As he neared the pile of firewood a cheer began to grow and grow. ❞

99

and halted at command. Every man was tearing himself loose, even Matthewson. Hats and mittens were flying in the air. Men were shaking hands, it did not matter with whom, and bubbling over in a general incoherent babel.

But Thornton fell on his knees beside Buck. Head was against head, and he was shaking him back and forth. Those who hurried up heard him cursing Buck and he cursed long and fervently, and softly and lovingly.

"Gad, sir! Gad, sir!" spluttered the Skookum Bench king. "I'll give a thousand for him, sir, a thousand, sir—twelve hundred sir."

Thornton rose to his feet. His eyes were wet. The tears were streaming frankly down his cheeks. "Sir," he said to the Skookum Bench king, "no sir. You can go to hell, sir. It's the best I can do for you, sir."

Buck seized Thornton's hand in his teeth. Thornton shook him back and forth. As though animated by a common impulse, the onlookers drew back to a respectful distance; nor were they again indiscreet enough to interrupt.

❝ Thornton fell on his knees beside Buck and he cursed long and fervently and softly and lovingly. **❞**

7

THE SOUNDING OF THE CALL

66 This lost mine was steeped in tragedy and shrouded in mystery. **99**

When Buck earned sixteen hundred dollars in five minutes for John Thornton, he made it possible for his master to pay off certain debts and to journey with his partners into the East after a fabled lost mine, the history of which was as old as the history of the country. Many men had sought it; few had found it; and more than a few there were who had never returned from the quest.

Prospectors pose for posterity in 1900. One of them holds a washing-pan, another a hunting gun, while the others play cards.

This lost mine was steeped in tragedy and shrouded in mystery. No one knew of the first man. The oldest tradition stopped before it got back to him. From the beginning there had been an ancient and ramshackle cabin. Dying men had sworn to it, and to the mine the site of which it marked, clinching their testimony with nuggets that were unlike any known grade of gold in the Northland.

But no living man had looted this treasure house and the dead were dead; wherefore John Thornton and Pete and Hans, with Buck and half a dozen other dogs, faced

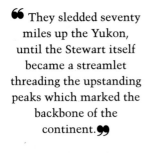

into the East on an unknown trail to achieve where men and dogs as good as themselves had failed. They sledded seventy miles up the Yukon, swung to the left into the Stewart River, passed the Mayo and the McQuestion, and held on until the Stewart itself became a streamlet, threading the upstanding peaks which marked the backbone of the continent.

John Thornton asked little of man or nature. He was unafraid of the wild. With a handful of salt and a rifle he could plunge into the wilderness and fare wherever he pleased and as long as he pleased. Being in no haste, Indian fashion, he hunted his dinner in the course of the day's travel; and if he failed to find it, like the Indian, he kept on traveling, secure in the knowledge that sooner or later he would come to it. So, on this great journey into the East, straight meat was the bill of fare, ammunition and tools principally made up the load on the sled, and the time-card was drawn upon the limitless future.

To Buck it was boundless delight, this hunting, fishing, and indefinite wandering through strange places. For weeks at a time they would hold on steadily, day after day; and for weeks upon end they would camp, here and there, the dogs loafing and

In this typical panorama of the Northern forest, a dense clump of conifers lines a river's shore.

102

the men burning holes through frozen muck and gravel and washing countless pans of dirt by the heat of the fire. Sometimes they went hungry, sometimes they feasted riotously, all according to the abundance of game and the fortune of hunting. Summer arrived, and dogs and men, packed on their backs, rafted across blue mountain lakes, and descended or ascended unknown rivers in slender boats whipsawed from the standing forest.

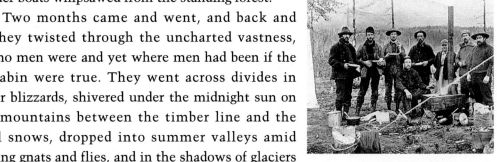

Two months came and went, and back and forth they twisted through the uncharted vastness, where no men were and yet where men had been if the Lost Cabin were true. They went across divides in summer blizzards, shivered under the midnight sun on naked mountains between the timber line and the eternal snows, dropped into summer valleys amid swarming gnats and flies, and in the shadows of glaciers picked strawberries and flowers as ripe and fair as any the Southland could boast. In the fall of the year they penetrated a weird lake country, sad and silent, where wild-fowl had been, but where then there was no life nor sign of life—only the blowing of chill winds, the forming of ice in sheltered places, and the melancholy rippling of waves on lonely beaches.

Meals were often the only moment of relaxation for the men, who gathered around the stove, each with his one and only plate. The moment they reached a town, the prospectors would rush to restaurants to feast on food and drink.

And through another winter they wandered on the obliterated trails of men who had gone before. Once, they came upon a path blazed through the forest, an ancient path, and the Lost Cabin seemed very near. But the path began nowhere and ended nowhere, and it remained mystery, as the man who made it and the reason he made it remained mystery. Another time they chanced upon the time-graven wreckage of a hunting lodge, and amid the shreds of rotted blankets John Thornton found a long-barreled flint-lock. He knew it for a Hudson Bay Company gun of the young days in the Northwest, when such a gun was worth its height in beaver skins packed flat. And that was all—

66 Summer arrived, and dogs and men rafted across blue mountain lakes.99

no hint as to the man who in an early day had reared the lodge and left the gun among the blankets.

Spring came on once more, and at the end of all their wandering they found, not the Lost Cabin, but a shallow placer in a broad valley where the gold showed like yellow butter across the bottom of the washing-pan. They sought no farther. Each day they worked earned them thousands of dollars in clean dust and nuggets, and they worked every day. The gold was sacked in moosehide bags, fifty pounds to/the bag, and piled like so much firewood outside the spruce-bough lodge. Like giants they toiled, days flashing on the heels of days like dreams as they heaped the treasure up.

The washing-pan is a steel receptacle with curved rims. Two-thirds filled with mud, it is immersed in the river and shaken. The sand and earth drain off, while nuggets of gold, being heavier, stay at the bottom.

There was nothing for the dogs to do, save the hauling in of meat now and again that Thornton killed, and Buck spent long hours musing by the fire. The vision of the short-legged hairy man came to him more frequently now that there was little work to be done; and often, blinking by the fire, Buck wandered with him in that other world which he remembered.

The salient thing of this other world seemed fear. When he watched the hairy man sleeping by the fire, head between his knees, and hands clasped above, Buck saw that he slept restlessly, with many starts and awakenings, at which times he would peer fearfully into the darkness and fling more wood upon the fire. Did they walk by the beach of a sea, where the hairy man gathered shell-fish and ate them as he gathered, it was with eyes that roved everywhere for hidden danger and with legs prepared to run like the wind at its first appearance. Through the forest they crept noiselessly, Buck at the hairy man's heels; and they were alert and vigilant, the pair of them, ears twitching and moving and nostrils quivering, for the man heard and smelled as keenly as Buck. The hairy man could spring up into the trees and travel ahead as fast as on the ground, swinging by the arms from limb to limb, sometimes a dozen feet apart, letting go and catching, never falling, never missing his grip. In fact, he seemed as much at home among the trees as on the ground; and Buck had memories of nights of vigil spent beneath trees wherein the hairy man roosted, holding on tightly as he slept.

Some Arctic peoples recount events by carving "story knives"; using the knifepoint, they draw a continuation of the story in the snow and recite it as well.

Each day they worked earned them thousands of dollars in clean dust and nuggets.

And closely akin to the visions of the hairy man was the call still sounding in the depths of the forest. It filled him with a great unrest and strange desires. It caused him to feel a vague, sweet gladness, and he was aware of wild yearnings and stirrings for he knew not what. Sometimes he pursued the call into the forest, looking for it as though it were a tangible thing, barking softly or defiantly, as the mood might dictate. He would thrust his nose into the cool wood moss, or into the black soil where long grasses grew, and snort with joy at the fat earth smells; or he would crouch for hours, as if in concealment, behind fungus-covered trunks of fallen trees, wide-eyed and wide-eared to all that moved and sounded about him. It might be, lying thus, that he hoped to surprise this call he could not understand. But he did not know why he did these various things. He was impelled to do them, and did not reason about them at all.

Irresistible impulses seized him. He would be lying in camp, dozing lazily in the heat of the day, when suddenly his head would lift and his ears cock up, intent and listening, and he would spring to his feet and dash away, and on and on, for hours, through the forest aisles and across the

The prospector's dream—to find nuggets, not just dust, at the bottom of a washing pan.

105

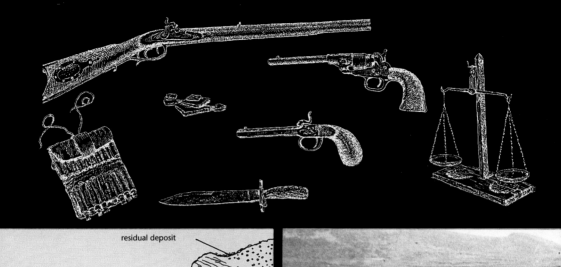

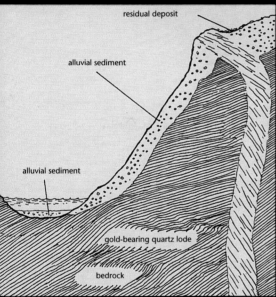

residual deposit

alluvial sediment

alluvial sediment

gold-bearing quartz lode

bedrock

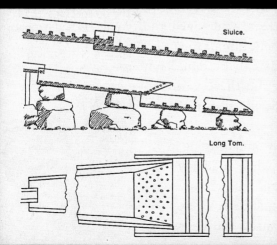

Sluice.

Long Tom.

The Quest for the Earth's Golden Fruits

Gold, which, mixed with quartz, lies deep in the subsoil, is gradually brought to the surface of the earth by the natural movement of layers of rock and sediment. As the mountains erode, countless waterways wearing away the surface sweep along gold specks and nuggets, creating deposits or alluvial sedimentation at the bottoms of rivers. Due to the shifting of the earth's crust, alluvial deposits can also be found in hillsides. There are therefore two ways of extracting gold: filtering the sand of a river by passing it through a sieve, sluice, "long Tom," or washing-pan, or digging out the mineral deposits to search for gold in them. In both cases, the prospectors need shovels, pickaxes, and hatchets—to work the riverbed, or to penetrate and then shore up the mine shafts. Or to save effort, they may just use dynamite.

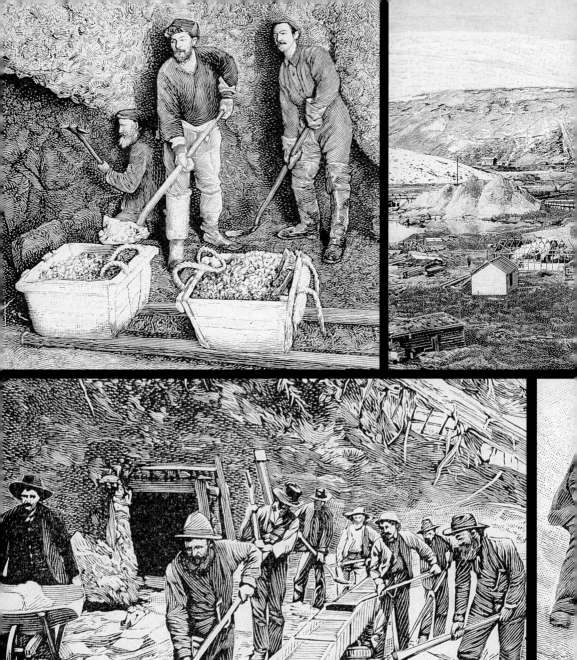

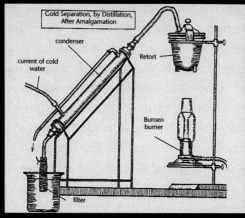

Gold Separation, by Distillation, After Amalgamation

condenser

current of cold water

Retort

Bunsen burner

filter

Extracting techniques

The apparatus shown opposite serves to separate the gold particles from pulverized quartz through a process called amalgamation. The retort, filled with a mixture of liquid mercury and quartz, is heated; the mercury and gold evaporate, separating from the quartz, and collect in the condenser; then this mixture is further distilled and the mercury evaporates leaving behind pure gold in the retort.

The prospectors' exhausting work was divided into several phases. First, a team loosened the quartz lodes in a mine shaft. The gold-bearing quartz gravel was loaded into wooden boxes that men pulled to the mine entrance. There, another team pulverized it—a gruelling task—and threw the gravel and ground mineral into the sluice, where a thin stream of water washed away the earth and gravel, allowing the gold to separate and sink to the bottom. The job required rerouting small streams, hence major carpentry work. Thus, extracting demanded considerable manpower, teamwork, and cooperation. Because of this necessary solidarity, prospecting led to the creation of unions and anarchist communities. In these lawless regions, the gold-miners were free to form small republics that elected their officials and shared supplies and profits.

109

66 One night he sprang from sleep with a start.**99**

open spaces where the niggerheads bunched. He loved to run down dry watercourses, and to creep and spy upon the bird life in the woods. For a day at a time he would lie in the underbrush where he could watch the partridges drumming and strutting up and down. But especially he loved to run in the dim twilight of the summer midnights, listening to the subdued and sleepy murmurs of the forest, reading signs and sounds as man may read a book, and seeking for the mysterious something that called—called, waking or sleeping, at all times, for him to come.

One night he sprang from sleep with a start, eager-eyed, nostrils quivering and scenting, his mane bristling in recurrent waves. From the forest came the call (or one note of it, for the call was many noted), distinct and definite as never before—a long-drawn howl, like, yet unlike, any noise made by husky dog. And he knew it, in the old familiar way, as a sound heard before. He sprang through the sleeping camp and in swift silence dashed through the woods. As he drew closer to the cry he went more slowly, with caution in every movement, till he came to an open place among the trees, and looking out, saw erect on haunches, with nose pointed to the sky, a long, lean timber wolf.

He had made no noise yet it ceased from its howling and tried to sense his presence. Buck stalked into the open, half crouching, body gathered compactly together, tail straight and stiff, feet falling with unwonted care. Every movement advertised commingled threatening and overture of friendliness. It was the menacing truce that marks the meeting of wild beasts that prey. But the wolf fled at sight of him. He followed, with wild leapings, in a frenzy to overtake. He ran him into a blind channel, in the bed of the creek, where a timber jam barred the way. The wolf whirled about, pivoting on his hind legs after the fashion of Joe and of all cornered husky dogs, snarling and bristling, clipping his teeth together in a continuous and rapid succession of snaps.

Buck did not attack, but circled about him and hedged him in with friendly advances. The wolf was suspicious and afraid; for Buck made three of him in

66 He came to an open place among the trees, and looking out, saw erect on haunches, with nose pointed to the sky, a long, lean timber wolf. 99

weight, while his head barely reached Buck's shoulder. Watching his chance, he darted away, and the chase was resumed. Time and again he was cornered, and the thing repeated, though he was in poor condition, or Buck could not so easily have overtaken him. He would run till Buck's head was even with the flank, when he would whirl around at bay, only to dash away again at the first opportunity.

But in the end Buck's pertinacity was rewarded; for the wolf, finding that no harm was intended, finally sniffed noses with him. Then they became friendly, and played about in the nervous, half-coy way with which fierce beasts belie their

66 It was the menacing truce that marks the meeting of wild beasts that prey. 99

❝ They ran side by side through the somber twilight. ❞

fierceness. After some time of this the wolf started off at an easy lope in a manner that plainly showed he was going somewhere. He made it clear to Buck that he was to come, and they ran side by side through the somber twilight, straight up the creek bed, into the gorge from which it issued, and across the bleak divide where it took its rise.

On the opposite slope of the watershed they came down into a level country where were great stretches of forest and many streams, and through these great stretches they ran steadily, hour after hour, the sun rising higher and the day growing warmer. Buck was wildly glad. He knew he was at last answering the call, running by the side of his wood brother toward the place from where the call surely came. Old memories were coming upon him fast, and he was stirring to them as of old he stirred to the realities of which they were the shadows. He had done this thing before, somewhere in that other and dimly remembered world, and he was doing it again, now, running free in the open, the unpacked earth underfoot, the wide sky overhead.

They stopped by a running stream to drink, and, stopping, Buck remembered John Thornton. He sat down. The wolf started on toward the place from where the call surely came, then returned to him, sniffing noses and making actions as though to encourage him. But Buck returned about and started slowly on the back track. For the better part of an hour the wild brother ran by his side, whining softly. Then he sat down, pointed his nose upward, and howled. It was a mournful howl, and as Buck held steadily on his way he heard it grow faint and fainter until it was lost in the distance.

John Thornton was eating dinner when Buck dashed into camp and sprang upon him in a frenzy of affection, overturning

him, scrambling upon him, licking his face, biting his hand—
"playing the general tom-fool," as John Thornton characterized it,
the while he shook Buck back and forth and cursed him lovingly.

For two days and nights Buck never left camp, never let
Thornton out of his sight. He followed him about his work,
watching him while he ate, saw him into his blankets at night
and out of them in the morning. But after two days the call in the
forest began to sound more imperiously than ever. Buck's
restlessness came back on him, and he was haunted by
recollections of the wild brother, and of the smiling land beyond
the divide and the run side by side through the wide forest
stretches. Once again he took to wandering in the woods, but the
wild brother came no more; and though he listened through long
vigils, the mournful howl was never raised.

He began to sleep out at night, staying away from camp
for days at a time; and once he crossed the divide at the head of
the creek and went down into the land of timber and streams.
There he wandered for a week, seeking vainly for fresh signs of
the wild brother, killing his meat as he traveled and traveling
with the long, easy lope that seems never to tire. He fished for
salmon in a broad stream that emptied somewhere into the sea,
and by this stream he killed a large black bear, blinded by the
mosquitoes while likewise fishing, and raging through the forest
helpless and terrible. Even so, it was a hard fight, and it aroused
the last latent remnants of Buck's ferocity. And two days later,
when he returned to his kill and found a dozen wolverines
quarreling over the spoil, he scattered them like chaff; and those
that fled left two behind who would quarrel no more.

The blood-longing became stronger than ever before. He
was a killer, a thing that preyed, living on the things that lived,
unaided, alone, by virtue of his own strength and prowess,

Wolves actually help
to keep the caribou
healthy. By attacking
weak or sick animals,
the predator
practices "natural
selection." Only the
strongest caribou
survive and breed.

113

surviving triumphantly in a hostile environment where only the strong survived. Because of all this he became possessed of a great pride in himself, which communicated itself like a contagion to his physical being. It advertised itself in all his movements, was apparent in the play of every muscle, spoke plainly as speech in the way he carried himself and made his glorious furry coat if anything more glorious. But for the stray brown on his muzzle and above his eyes, and for the splash of white hair that ran midmost down his chest, he might well have been mistaken for a gigantic wolf, larger than the largest of the breed. From his St. Bernard father he had inherited size and weight, but it was his shepherd mother who had given shape to that size and weight. His muzzle was the long wolf muzzle, save that it was larger than the muzzle of any wolf; and his head, somewhat broader, was the wolf head on a massive scale.

> **❝** The moose appeared in greater abundance, moving slowly down to meet the winter in the lower and less rigorous valleys. **❞**

The caribou is perfectly adapted to the tundra and taiga. Its very broad side hoofs allow it to move over soft or slippery terrain as well as to pierce icy surfaces in order to get to the moss and lichen buried beneath.

His cunning was wolf cunning, and the wild cunning; his intelligence, shepherd intelligence and St. Bernard intelligence; and all this, plus an experience gained in the fiercest of schools, made him as formidable a creature as any that roamed the wild. A carnivorous animal, living on a straight meat diet, he was in full flower, at the high tide of his life, overspilling with vigor and virility. When Thornton passed a caressing hand along his back, a snapping and cracking followed the hand, each hair discharging its pent magnetism at the contact. Every part, brain and body, nerve tissue and fiber, was keyed to the most exquisite pitch; and between all the parts there was a perfect equilibrium or adjustment. To sights and sounds and events which required action, he responded with lightning-like rapidity. Quickly as a husky dog could leap to defend from attack or to attack, he could leap twice as quickly. He saw the movement, or heard the sound, and responded in less time than another dog required to compass the mere seeing or hearing. He perceived and determined and

responded in the same instant. In point of fact the three actions of perceiving, determining, and responding were sequential; but so infinitesimal were the intervals of time between them that they appeared simultaneous. His muscles were surcharged with vitality, and snapped into play sharply, like steel springs. Life streamed through him in splendid flood, glad and rampant, until it seemed that it would burst him asunder in sheer ecstasy and pour forth generously over the world.

"Never was there such a dog," said John Thornton one day as the partners watched Buck marching out of camp.

"When he was made, the mold was broke," said Pete.

"Py jingo! I t'ink so mineself," Hans affirmed.

They saw him marching out of camp, but they did not see the instant and terrible transformation which took place as soon as he was within the secrecy of the forest. He no longer marched. At once he became a thing of the wild, stealing along softly, cat-footed, a passing shadow that appeared and dis-

The moose lives in the Northern wilderness. In good weather, it lives by lakes and streams, where it eats great quantities of aquatic plants.

❝ Buck proceeded to cut the bull out from the herd. **❞**

The reunions of members of a wolf pack are an occasion for great shows of joy. The creatures rub against their leader and greet each other with copious licking.

appeared among the shadows. He knew how to take advantage of every cover, to crawl on his belly like a snake, and like a snake to leap and strike. He could take a ptarmigan from its nest, kill a rabbit as it slept, and snap in mid air the little chipmunks fleeing a second too late for the trees. Fish, in open pools, were not too quick for him; nor were beaver, mending their dams, too wary. He killed to eat, not from wantonness; but he preferred to eat what he killed himself. So a lurking humor ran through his deeds, and it was his delight to steal upon the squirrels, and, when he all but had them, to let them go, chattering in mortal fear to the tree-tops.

As the fall of the year came on the moose appeared in greater abundance, moving slowly down to meet the winter in the lower and less rigorous valleys. Buck had already dragged down a stray part-grown calf; but he wished strongly for larger and more formidable quarry, and he came upon it one day on the divide at the head of the creek. A bank of twenty moose had crossed over from the land of streams and timber, and chief among them was a great bull. He was in a savage temper, and, standing over six feet from the ground, was as formidable an antagonist as even Buck could desire. Back and forth the bull tossed his great palmated antlers, branching to fourteen points and embracing seven feet within the tips. His small eyes burned with a vicious and bitter light, while he roared with fury at sight of Buck.

From the bull's side, just forward of the flank, protruded a

feathered arrow-end, which accounted for his savageness. Guided by that instinct which came from the old hunting days of the primordial world, Buck proceeded to cut the bull out from the herd. It was no slight task. He would bark and dance about in front of the bull, just out of reach of the great antlers and of the terrible splay hoofs which could have stamped his life out with a single blow. Unable to turn his back on the fanged danger and go on, the bull would be driven into paroxysms of rage. At such moments he charged Buck, who retreated craftily, luring him on by a simulated

66 At last, at the end of the fourth day, he pulled the great moose down. **99**

Leaps and simulated combat, designed to show off the participants' strength and agility, are a regular part of Indian dancing in the Northwest.

inability to escape. But when he was thus separated from his fellows, two or three of the younger bulls would charge back upon Buck and enable the wounded bull to rejoin the herd.

There is a patience of the wild—dogged, tireless, persistent as life itself—that holds motionless for endless hours the spider in its web, the snake in its coils, the panther in its ambuscade; this patience belongs peculiarly to life when it hunts its living food; and it belonged to Buck as he clung to the flank of the herd, retarding its march, irritating the young bulls, worrying the cows with their half-grown calves, and driving the wounded bull mad with helpless rage. For half a day this continued. Buck multiplied himself, attacking from all sides, enveloping the herd in a whirlwind of menace, cutting out his victim as fast as it could rejoin its mates, wearing out the patience of creatures preyed upon, which is a lesser patience than that of creatures preying.

As the day wore along and the sun dropped to its bed in the northwest (the darkness had come back and the fall nights were six hours long), the young bulls retraced their steps more and more reluctantly to the aid of their beset leader. The down-coming winter was harrying them on to the lower levels, and it seemed they could never shake off this tireless creature that held them back. Besides, it was not the life of the herd, or of the young bulls, that was threatened. The life of only one member was demanded, which was a remoter interest than their lives, and in the end they were content to pay the toll.

As twilight fell the old bull stood with lowered head, watching his mates—the cows he had known, the calves he had fathered, the bulls he had mastered—as they shambled on at a rapid pace through the fading light. He could not follow, for before his nose leaped the merciless fanged terror that would not let him go. Three hundred-weight more than half a ton he weighed; he had lived a long, strong life, full of fight and struggle, and at the end he faced death at the teeth of a creature whose head did not reach beyond his great knuckled knees.

From then on, night and day, Buck never left his prey, never gave it a moment's rest, never permitted it to browse the leaves of the trees or the shoots of young birch and willow. Nor did he give the wounded bull opportunity to slake his burning thirst in the slender trickling streams they crossed. Often, in desperation, he burst into long stretches of flight. At such times Buck did not attempt to stay him, but loped easily at his heels, satisfied with the way the game was played, lying down when the moose stood

66 Buck peered out where the spruce-bough lodge had been and saw what made his hair leap straight up on his neck and shoulders. **99**

119

still, attacking him fiercely when he strove to eat or drink.

The great head drooped more and more under its tree of horns, and the shambling trot grew weaker and weaker. He took to standing for long periods, with nose to the ground and dejected ears dropped limply; and Buck found more time in which to get water for himself and in which to rest. At such moments, panting with red lolling tongue and with eyes fixed upon the big bull, it appeared to Buck that a change was coming over the face of things. He could feel a new stir in the land. As the moose were coming into the land, other kinds of life were coming in. Forest and stream and air seemed palpitant with their presence. The news of it was borne in upon him, not by sight, or sound, or smell, but by some other and subtler sense. He heard nothing, saw nothing, yet knew that the land was somehow different; that through it strange things were afoot and ranging; and he resolved to investigate after he had finished the business in hand.

At last, at the end of the fourth day, he pulled the great moose down. For a day and a night he remained by the kill, eating and sleeping, turn and turn about. Then, rested, refreshed and strong, he turned his face toward camp and John Thornton. He broke into the long easy lope, and went on, hour after hour, never at loss for the tangled way, heading straight home through strange country with a certitude of direction that put man and his magnetic needle to shame.

As he held on he became more and more conscious of the new stir in the land. There was life abroad in it different from the life which had been there throughout the summer. No longer was this fact borne in upon him in some subtle, mysterious way. The birds talked of it, the squirrels chattered about it, the very breeze whispered of it. Several times he stopped and drew in the fresh morning air in great sniffs, reading a message which made him leap on with greater speed. He was oppressed with a sense of calamity happening, if it were not calamity already happened; and as he crossed the last watershed and dropped down into the valley toward camp, he proceeded with great caution.

Three miles away he came upon a fresh trail that sent his

neck hair rippling and bristling. It led straight toward camp and John Thornton. Buck hurried on, swiftly and stealthily, every nerve straining and tense, alert to the multitudinous details which told a story— all but the end. His nose gave him a varying description of the passage of the life on the heels of which he was traveling. He remarked the pregnant silence of the forest. The bird life had flitted. The squirrels were in hiding. One only he saw—a sleek gray fellow, flattened against a gray dead limb so that he seemed a part of it, a woody excresence upon the wood itself.

As Buck slid along with the obscureness of a gliding shadow, his nose was jerked suddenly to the side as though a positive force had gripped and pulled it. He followed the new scent into a thicket and found Nig. He was lying on his side, dead where he had dragged himself, an arrow protruding, head and feathers, from either side of his body.

A hundred yards farther on, Buck came upon one of the sled-dogs Thornton had bought in Dawson. This dog was thrashing about in a death-struggle, directly on the trail, and Buck passed around him without stopping. From the camp came the faint sound of many voices, rising and falling in a sing-song chant. Bellying forward to the edge of the clearing, he found Hans, lying on his face, feathered with arrows like a porcupine. At the same instant Buck peered out where the spruce-bough lodge had been and saw what made his hair leap straight up on his neck and shoulders. A gust of overpowering rage swept over him. He did not know that he growled, but he growled aloud with a terrible ferocity. For the last time in his life he allowed passion to usurp cunning and

66 All day Buck brooded by the pool or roamed restlessly about the camp. **99**

121

reason, and it was because of his great love for John Thornton that he lost his head.

The Yeehats were dancing about the wreckage of the spruce-bough lodge when they heard a fearful roaring and saw rushing upon them an animal the like of which they had never seen before. It was Buck, a live hurricane of fury, hurling himself upon them in a frenzy to destroy. He sprang at the foremost man (it was the chief of the Yeehats), ripping the throat wide open till the rent jugular spouted a fountain of blood. He did not pause to worry the victim, but ripped in passing, with the next bound tearing wide the throat of a second man. There was no withstanding him. He plunged about in their very midst, tearing, rending, destroying, in constant and terrific motion which defied the arrows they discharged at him. In fact, so inconceivably rapid were his movements, and so closely were the Indians tangled together, that they shot one another with the arrows; and one young hunter, hurling a spear at Buck in midair, drove it through the chest of another hunter with such force that the point broke through the skin of the back and stood out beyond. Then a panic seized the Yeehats, and they fled in terror to the woods, proclaiming as they fled the advent of the Evil Spirit.

And truly Buck was the Fiend incarnate, raging at their

> **"** And now the call came to Buck in unmistakable accents. He, too, sat down and howled. The pack crowded around him, sniffing in half-friendly, half-savage manner. **"**

heels and dragging them down like deer as they raced through the trees. It was a fateful day for the Yeehats. They scattered far and wide over the country, and it was not till a week later that the last of the survivors gathered together in a lower valley and counted their losses. As for Buck, wearying of the pursuit, he returned to the desolated camp. He found Pete where he had been killed in his blankets in the first moment of surprise. Thornton's desperate struggle was fresh-written on the earth, and Buck scented every detail of it down to the edge of a deep pool. By the edge, head and forefeet in the water, lay Skeet, faithful to the last. The pool itself, muddy and discoloured from the sluice boxes, effectually hid what it contained, and it contained John Thornton; for Buck followed his trace into the water, from which no trace led away.

All day Buck brooded by the pool or roamed restlessly about the camp. Death, as a cessation of movement, as a passing out and away from the lives of the living, he knew, and he knew that John Thornton was dead. It left a great void in him, somewhat akin to hunger, but a void which ached and ached, and which food could not fill. At times when he paused to contemplate the carcasses of the Yeehats, he forgot the pain of it; and at such times he was aware of a great pride in himself—a pride greater than any he had yet experienced. He had killed man, the noblest game of all, and he had killed in the face of the law of club and fang. He sniffed the bodies curiously. They had died so easily. It was harder to kill a husky dog than them. They were no match at all, were it not for their arrows and spears and clubs. Thenceforward he would be unafraid of them except when they bore in their hands their arrows, spears, and clubs.

Night came on, and a full moon rose high over the trees into the sky, lighting the land till it lay bathed in ghostly day. And with the coming of the night, brooding and mourning by the pool, Buck became alive to a stirring of the new life in the forest other than that which the Yeehats had made. He

stood up, listening and scenting. From far away drifted a faint, sharp yelp, followed by a chorus of similar sharp yelps. As the moments passed the yelps grew closer and louder. Again Buck knew them as things heard in that other world which persisted in his memory. He walked to the center of the open space and listened. It was the call, the many-noted call, sounding more luringly and compellingly than ever before. And as never before, he was ready to obey. John Thornton was dead. The last tie was

broken. Man and the claims of man no longer bound him.

Hunting their living meat, as the Yeehats were hunting it, on the flanks of the migrating moose, the wolf pack had at last crossed over from the land of streams and timber and invaded Buck's valley. Into the clearing where the moonlight streamed, they poured in a silvery flood; and in the center of the clearing stood Buck, motionless as a statue, waiting their coming. They were awed, so still and large he stood, and a moment's pause fell, till the boldest one leaped straight for him. Like a flash Buck struck, breaking the neck. Then he stood, without movement, as before, the stricken wolf rolling in agony behind him. Three others tried it in sharp succession; and one after the other they drew back, streaming blood from slashed throats or shoulders.

This was sufficient to fling the whole pack forward, pell-

mell, crowded together, blocked and confused by its eagerness to pull down the prey. Buck's marvelous quickness and agility stood him in good stead. Pivoting on his hind legs, and snapping and gashing, he was everywhere at once, presenting a front which was apparently unbroken so swiftly did he whirl and guard from side to side. But to prevent them from getting behind him, he was forced back, down past the pool and into the creek bed, till he brought up against a high gravel bank. He worked along to a right angle in the bank which the men had made in the course of mining, and in this angle he came to bay, protected on three sides and with nothing to do but face the front.

And so well did he face it, that at the end of half an hour the wolves drew back discomfited. The tongues of all were out and lolling, the white fangs showing cruelly white in the moonlight. Some were lying down with heads raised and ears pricked forward; others stood on their feet, watching him; and still others were lapping water from the pool. One wolf, long and lean and grey, advanced cautiously, in a friendly manner, and Buck recognized the wild brother with whom he had run for a night and day. He was whining softly and, as Buck whined, they touched noses.

Then an old wolf, gaunt and battle-scarred, came forward. Buck writhed his lips into the preliminary of a snarl, but sniffed noses with him. Whereupon the old wolf sat down, pointed nose at the moon, and broke out the long wolf howl. The others sat down and howled. And now the call came to Buck in unmistakable accents. He, too, sat down and howled. This over, he came out of his angle and the pack crowded around him, sniffing in half-friendly, half-savage manner. The leaders lifted the yelp of the pack and sprang away into the woods. The wolves swung in behind yelping in chorus. And Buck ran with them, side by side with the wild brother, yelping as he ran.

And here may well end the story of Buck. The years were not many when the Yeehats noted a change in the breed of timber wolves; for some were seen with splashes of brown on head and muzzle, and with a rift of white centring down the chest. But more remarkable than this, the Yeehats tell of a Ghost Dog that runs at the head of the pack. They are afraid of this

Ghost Dog, for it has cunning greater than they, stealing from their camps in fierce winters, robbing their traps, slaying their dogs, and defying the bravest hunters.

Nay, the tale grows worse. Hunters there are who fail to return to the camp, and hunters there have been whom their tribesmen found with throats slashed cruelly open and with wolf prints about them in the snow greater than the prints of any wolf. Each fall, when the Yeehats follow the movement of the moose, there is a certain valley which they never enter. And women there are who become sad when the word goes over the fire of how the Evil Spirit came to select that valley for an abiding-place.

In the summers there is one visitor, however, to that valley, of which the Yeehats do not know. It is a great, gloriously coated wolf, like, and yet unlike, all other wolves. He crosses alone from the smiling timber land and comes down into an open space among the trees. Here a yellow stream flows from rotted moose-hide sacks and sinks into the ground, with long grasses growing through it and vegetable mold overrunning it and hiding its yellow from the sun; and here he muses for a time, howling once, long and mournfully, ere he departs.

But he is not always alone. When the long winter nights come on and the wolves follow their meat into the lower valleys, he may be seen running at the head of the pack, through the pale moonlight or glimmering borealis, leaping gigantic above his fellows, his great throat a-bellow as he sings a song of the younger world, which is the song of the pack.

VIKING
Published by the Penguin Group
Penguin Books USA Inc., 375 Hudson Street, New York, New York 10014, U.S.A.
Penguin Books Ltd, 27 Wrights Lane, London W8 5TZ, England
Penguin Books Australia Ltd, Ringwood, Victoria, Australia
Penguin Books Canada Ltd, 10 Alcorn Avenue, Toronto, Ontario, Canada M4V 3B2
Penguin Books (N.Z.) Ltd, 182–190 Wairau Road, Auckland 10, New Zealand

Penguin Books Ltd, Registered Offices: Harmondsworth, Middlesex, England

First published in 1903
Published with illustrations in 1994 by Éditions Gallimard
Published in 1996 by Viking, a division of Penguin Books USA Inc.

1 3 5 7 9 10 8 6 4 2

Copyright © Éditions Gallimard, 1994
Notes by Philippe Jacquin
Illustrations by Philippe Munch
Note translation by David Jacobson

All rights reserved

Library of Congress Catalog Card Number: 95-61728
ISBN 0-670-86918-X

Printed in Italy
Set in Trump Mediaeval

PHOTO CREDITS

Antarctica Photo Agency 37, 56. Archives Gallimard, Paris 104 top, 105 bottom. Bios, Paris 32, 114. Bios/C. Sourd 53. Bios/Denis Bringard 28, 49. Bios/Henry Ausloos 23. Bios/Klein & Hubert 48 top & bottom, 54, 113, 116. Bios/O. Langrand 42. All rights reserved, 7, 10, 11 top, 11 bottom, 12, 13 middle left, 15, 16, 17, 18, 19, 20, 30 bottom right, 31 bottom right, 31 top, 38, 50/51, 50 bottom, 50 middle, 51 bottom, 63 bottom, 65, 78, 82, 83, 91, 107 bottom right, 108 top left, 109 middle right. Ciné-Plus, Paris 31 lower left. Dagli Orti, Paris 104 bottom. Explorer, Vanves 62 top. Hulton-Deutsch Collection, London 13 middle right, 73. Jacana/F.S. Balthis, Paris 86, 102. Jacana/St. Krasemann, Paris 80 top, 81. Jacana/Tom Walker, Paris 80 bottom. Jean-Loup Charmet, Paris 13 upper right. Jean Vigne, Gennevilliers 30 bottom left, 36, 61, 62 bottom. Kharbine-Tapabour, Paris 8 top, 14, 40. Mary Evans Picture Library, London 16 top, 31 bottom right, 60 top and bottom, 98, 108 upper middle, 108 bottom, 108/109 top, 108/109 bottom. Musée de l'homme, Paris 27, 120 top and bottom. Musée de l'homme/D. Estable, Paris 59. Musée de l'homme/Gessain, Paris 63 top, 71, 74. Musée de l'homme/Michéa, Paris 52 bottom, 64, 70, 76, 77. Musée de la vénerie, Senlis 88. Museum national d'histoire naturelle, Paris 26, 41. Peter Newark, Bath 13 bottom, 24, 30 top, 33, 68, 94, 97, 106/107. Pix-Beignet, Paris 9. Roger-Viollet, Paris 52 top, 92 bottom, 101, 115. Russ Kingman, Glen Ellen 13 top left, 67, 92 top, 96, 103. Smithsonian, National Archeological Archives, Washington D.C. 118. The Bettmann Archives, New York, 8 bottom, 35, 47, 58 top. Transantartica/F. Latreille 29. University of Washington, Special Collections Division Library 75.

ACKNOWLEDGMENTS

Éditions Gallimard wishes to thank Mrs. Russ Kingman for her help in providing historical images.

Éditions Gallimard
Director : Pierre Marchand
Editor : Cécile Dutheil de la Rochère
Project Manager : Béatrice Jaulin
Picture Research : Nathalie Bréaud
Layout : François Chentrier
Copyeditors : Annabelle Viret and Evelyne Pezzopane

Viking
Editors : Lisa Bernstein and Melanie Cecka
Design : Margaret Mirabile and Nina Putignano
Production Editor : Janet Pascal

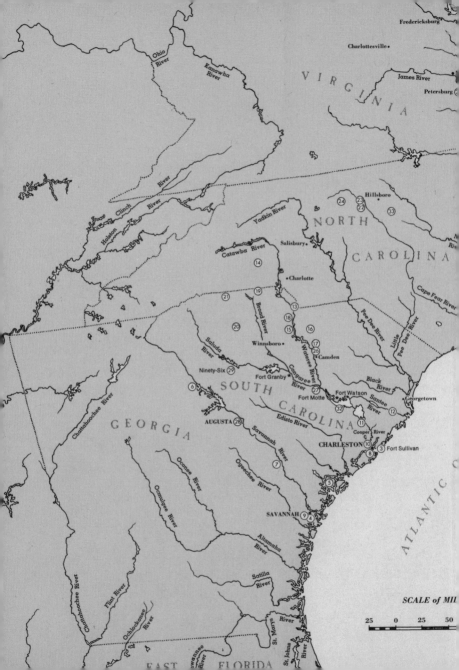

76, 80; flees to Lancaster and York (Pa.),
89; 91, 92; issues letters of marque, 96;
commissions warships, 97; 106, 109,
112, 119; votes bonus to soldiers, 122
Serapis (HMS), *98*, 99
Serres, Dominique (artist), *74*
Sheftall, Mordecai, 62
Short, Richard (artist), *53*
Slavery, mentioned in first draft of Declaration of Independence, 58, 63
Sons of Liberty, 18
Spain, declares war on Britain, 103
Stamp Act, 18
Staten Island (N.Y.), *54*, 70
Steuben, Maj. Gen. Friedrich Wilhelm
Augustus, Baron von, at Valley Forge,
93; in Virginia, 117
Stillwater (N.Y.), 86
Stirling, Brig. Gen. Lord (William Alexander),
67
Stuart kings, 46
Sullivan, Maj. Gen. John, 64, 66, 69; at
Newport (R.I.), 96
Sullivan's Island (Charleston, S.C.), 51, 52,
107
Susquehanna River, 92

TARLETON, Col. Banastre, 110, 113, 114
Thomas, Maj. Gen. John, 48, 53, 54
Tories (Loyalists), 45, 46, 47, 50, 52, 58,
59, 64, 84, 92, 95, 101, 103, 110, 114,
115
Townshend Acts, 18
Trenton (N.J.), 76, 77, 78
Trevelyan, Sir George Otto, 69
Trumbull, John (artist), *31*, *40-41*, *56-57*,
120-121
Trumbull (USS), 99

UNANIMOUS Declaration (Declaration of
Independence), *56*, *57*, 58, 60, *61*, 70

VALCOUR Bay (Lake Champlain), Battle of,
72-73, 74
Valley Forge (Pa.), 62, 90; winter at, *91*;
106
Vincennes, surrender of, *100*, 102
Virginia Assembly, 19

WABASH River, 102
Ward, Maj. Gen. Artemas, 28, 30
Washington, Gen. George, chosen to lead
army 30, 31; takes command 35, 36;
plans Quebec expedition, 39; 41, 48, 50,
51, 54, 56; largest number in army of,
58; orders Declaration read to army, 60;
use of Indians, 62; accepts Negro recruits
63; 65; at Battle of Long Island, 67; 68,
69, 70; to White Plains, 71; 72, *74*, *75*,
76; victory at Trenton, 77; 78, 79, 80, 82,
83; at Brandywine, 88-89; 90; at Valley
Forge, 91 *ff*; at Monmouth, 95; 96, 97,
101, 103, 105; at Morristown, 106; 107;
faces mutiny, 108; 109, 110, 112, 116;
moves South, 117; 118, 119
Wasp (USS), 98
Westchester (N.Y.), 71
West Indies, 74, 96, 104, 118
West Point (N.Y.), 116
Whipple, Prince, 63
Whitehaven (England), 99
White Plains (N.Y.), 71, 96
Wilderness Road, 101
Wilmington (N.C.), 47, 115
Women in Revolution, 64
"World Turned Upside Down, The," 118
Wright, Mrs. David, 64

YOHN, F. C. (artist), *11*, *51*, *88-89*, *100*,
111, *116*
York (Pa.), 89
Yorktown (Va.), 117, *120-121*